SUBVERTING
the REPUBLIC

HOW THE 17TH AMENDMENT AND CITIZENS UNITED CORRUPTED THE BALANCE OF AMERICAN GOVERNMENT

STEVEN BRADLEY

Subverting the Republic

Subverting the Republic: How the 17th Amendment and Citizens United Corrupted the Balance of American Government

Published by **SCBradley Publishing**
North Richland Hills, Texas
www.SubvertingTheRepublic.com

Library of Congress Control Number: **2025912017**
ISBN: **979-8-218-70783-5**

Printed in the United States of America
Cover and interior design by SCBradley Publishing
First Edition – July 4, 2025

CONTENTS

Visit SubvertingTheRepublic.com for extended source files, visuals, and interactive materials.

DEDICATION

To **my wife, Lake Bradley** — the wisest person I know. A seventh-generation Texan whose family heritage runs as deep and wide as my own, she is the unwavering heart behind this entire project. Her courage, clarity, and burning love for both this nation and the Republic of Texas have been my compass. Her devotion to scriptural truth, her passionate defense of liberty, and her steadfast belief in me — even when the road was uncertain — made this book not only possible, but inevitable.

To my children, **Lynwood**, **Andrew**, and **Alexander** — may you always know the richness of your inheritance, not in gold, but in grit, faith, and the freedom to stand upright in a world that wants you to kneel.

To my parents, **Lester Carl Bradley** and my late mother, **Carol Ann Honaker Bradley**, who raised me with reverence for truth and the quiet, defiant love of country that never apologizes for believing in the Founders' intent.

To my brothers, **Gerald Allen Bradley** and the late **Mark Eden Bradley** — whose loyalty and memory continue to shape my resolve.

And last, but not least, to **my dear friend William** — the voice of reason and resilience behind this project. This book could never have been written without the invaluable assistance of my friend, whose knowledge and common-sense understanding of this national experiment is without measure.

ACKNOWLEDGMENTS

Special thanks to:

- The anonymous attorneys, researchers, and historians who contributed behind the scenes
- Every patriot, content creator, independent journalist, and local organizer fighting for a freer future
- The framers and philosophers quoted throughout: Madison, Jefferson, Hamilton, Paine, Franklin, Spooner, Locke, and King
- My early readers and critics who helped refine each argument with clarity and conviction

Watch for my next book: **"The Sons of Dan: Tracing the Lost Tribe through the American Frontier"**, a fictional exploration of ancestral lines, prophecy, and the birth of liberty-minded peoples across nations.

FOREWORD

They say history doesn't repeat, but it often rhymes.

What you're about to read isn't just a book—it's a warning. A map. And perhaps, a spark.

I didn't set out to write Subverting the Republic with the intent of becoming an author. I'm an entrepreneur, a builder by nature—of things, of systems, of solutions. But I'm also a son of Appalachia, raised by coal miners and preachers, by men who spoke plainly and women who remembered everything. I was taught to value hard work, truth spoken without fear, and the quiet strength of those who stood their ground even when the ground was being taken from under them.

As I studied our Constitution and its transformation over time, I began to notice a pattern—a subtle unraveling that began over a century ago. Laws passed under noble slogans had, in practice, stripped away the very balance that made this nation unique. Amendments meant to "modernize" our government weakened the voice of the states. Court decisions meant to "protect speech" empowered the rich to drown out the rest of us.

The 17th Amendment. The Federal Reserve Act. The 16th Amendment. And nearly a hundred years later, Citizens United. Each a step in a quiet coup not waged by foreign powers, but by domestic interests with deep pockets and even deeper intentions.

I do not write from a partisan place. I write as a citizen who still believes in the vision of our founders—a republic of checks and balances, of state sovereignty, of equal voice, and accountable government. I believe we have not lost that republic. But we are losing it.

This book is the result of years of study, decades of quiet reflection, and a lifetime of living in the shadow of what once was. It's a challenge to both the left and the right. It's a call to return—not to nostalgia or fantasy—but to structural integrity, to the scaffolding that once held our system upright.

Whether you are a judge, a legislator, a voter, or a student of history, I ask only that you read with open eyes and a willing heart. You may not agree with everything here, and that's fine. But if this work sparks a question, or a doubt, or even a desire to look deeper, then it will have done its job.

This is not the end of a conversation. It's the beginning of a reckoning.

—Steven Bradley
Summer, 2025

INDEX & BIBLIOGRAPHY

(Selections)

- **Federalist Papers**, Nos. 10, 39, 46, 51 (James Madison, Alexander Hamilton)
- **Declaration of Independence** (1776)
- **U.S. Constitution** (Original and Amendments)
- **Lysander Spooner**, *No Treason: The Constitution of No Authority* (1867)
- **G. Edward Griffin**, *The Creature from Jekyll Island* (1994)
- **Thomas Paine**, *Common Sense* (1776)
- **John Locke**, *Second Treatise of Government* (1689)
- **Martin Luther King Jr.**, *Letter from Birmingham Jail* (1963)
- **Citizens United v. FEC**, 558 U.S. 310 (2010)
- **McCutcheon v. FEC**, 572 U.S. 185 (2014)
- **Printz v. United States**, 521 U.S. 898 (1997)

For a full digital bibliography and extended source archive, visit **SubvertingTheRepublic.com/resources**

PREFACE

The Bloodline of a Republic

There is a weight that settles on your chest when you realize the country you love is no longer what it claims to be.

My name is Steven Bradley, and this book is not merely a political critique or historical summary — it is a personal reckoning. It is the product of a lifelong struggle to understand how the republic handed down by our forefathers was quietly, deliberately, and systematically subverted.

I come from a long line of Americans who helped build and defend this nation — not metaphorically, but literally. On my father's side, **Thomas Bradley II** arrived in the colonies between **1653 and 1655**. From that moment forward, **every generation of my family has fought in every American war**, from before the Revolution to the modern day.

On my mother's side, **Jans Jacob Honaker** came to this country in **1749** and **served in the Revolutionary War**. His descendants, too, have defended this land in every conflict since. In fact, many of the rifles carried by the pioneers — those who declared our independence and fought to preserve it — were **Honaker rifles**, handcrafted by my ancestors.

This book, then, is written not just by a student of history or a frustrated citizen. It is written by someone whose bloodlines run through the very marrow of this country. I write not out of partisanship, but because I cannot stay silent while the constitutional framework they bled for is dismantled — not by force, but by finance.

We are told we live in a democracy. We are told our votes matter, our voices count, and that the government exists to serve us.

But those of us paying attention know better.

We are no longer a **Compound Republic**, as James Madison envisioned — a layered structure of authority balancing federal and state powers, designed to keep tyranny at bay. That structure has been quietly eroded through constitutional amendments, judicial rulings, and unchecked campaign finance practices — all culminating in a system **far more reminiscent of aristocracy or monarchy than republican self-governance**.

The erosion began with the **17th Amendment**, which stripped state legislatures of their voice in the federal government. It accelerated with the **Federal Reserve Act** and the **16th Amendment**, centralizing economic power in the hands of unelected bankers and bureaucrats. And it was sealed by **Citizens United**, which turned money into speech and handed the reins of influence to those with the deepest pockets.

This is not a partisan book. It is a **constitutional alarm** — a call for clarity, for courage, and for citizens of all political stripes to recognize that the republic has been hijacked by interests far removed from the people.

If you feel it too — that deep unease, that sense that something sacred has been lost — then this book is for you.

EXCERPT FROM BOOK TRAILER SCRIPT

[Scene: Fading images of Revolutionary War soldiers, black powder rifles, parchment documents. The words "A Republic, if you can keep it..." echo as Benjamin Franklin's voice fades into static.]

Narrator (voice-over):

It began as the greatest experiment in self-government the world had ever seen — a nation built not on bloodlines or crowns, but on consent and balance.

[Scene: News clips flash. Super PAC logos. Dollar signs. Senators shaking hands with lobbyists.]

Narrator:

But over time, the safeguards were dismantled. State power erased. Campaigns bought and sold. Citizens silenced by the roar of corporate speech.

[Scene: The Capitol fades into a fortress. Faint red, white, and blue overlay with growing shadows.]

Narrator:

In 1913, they opened the gates. In 2010, they sealed them shut.

[Scene: Close-up of the Constitution being slowly burned from the edges. In bold letters, the words "17th Amendment" and "Citizens United" emerge.]

Narrator:

We were warned — by Madison, by Jefferson, by Lincoln. The republic would not be lost to foreign invasion, but from within.

[Scene: Silence. A young man places a folded American flag into a wooden box. A tear falls.]

Narrator (softly):

But the torch hasn't gone out. The fight is not over. It's time to restore the republic.

[Text on screen: *Subverting the Republic: How the 17th Amendment and Citizens United Corrupted the Balance of American Government*] *Available now.*

CLOSING: A CALL TO ACTION

This book will challenge you. It will confront what you think you know about democracy, representation, and power in America.

But it will also offer hope — the kind of hope that grows not from slogans or speeches, but from **civic clarity and historical understanding**.

If we are to restore the balance our ancestors fought for, we must first understand how it was taken from us. And then — with determination, unity, and courage — we must take it back.

The republic is still within reach. But only if we fight for it now.

INTRODUCTION

The Republic We Lost

"A Republic, if you can keep it."

— Benjamin Franklin

For most Americans, democracy is taken for granted. It is pledged in our classrooms, echoed in our political speeches, and assumed in every conversation about "freedom." We are taught that every citizen has a voice, every vote counts, and the government exists to serve us — the people.

But the sobering truth is this: **we do not live in the democracy we believe we have.**

We live under the **illusion of democracy**, carefully maintained through ceremony and media, while the true levers of power have been seized by a **permanent, unaccountable oligarchy**. The names of the politicians may change, but the money behind them does not. The issues may rotate, but the outcomes remain eerily consistent: the rich get richer, government gets larger, and the voice of the average American grows quieter.

How did we arrive here? The answer is not found in the last election or even the last administration — but in a century-long unraveling of the very structure our Founders designed to prevent exactly this kind of consolidation.

A REPUBLIC, NOT A DEMOCRACY

The Founders did not create a democracy. They were, in fact, deeply suspicious of it. To them, democracy meant mob rule — the tyranny of the majority. As James Madison wrote in *Federalist No. 10*, democracies are "spectacles of turbulence and contention" and are "incompatible with personal security or the rights of property."

Instead, they gave us a **Compound Republic** — a system of divided sovereignty and overlapping jurisdictions. Power would be balanced between the federal government and the states, between the House and the Senate, between the executive and the legislature, and ultimately between the people and their representatives. This structure was not accidental. It was **intentional by design** — a safeguard against corruption, ambition, and centralized control.

Every element of this system had a purpose:

- The **House of Representatives** would speak directly for the people.

- The **Senate**, chosen by state legislatures, would represent the interests of the sovereign states.
- The **President** would be indirectly elected by an Electoral College, providing an additional buffer from popular passions.
- And the **Supreme Court** would stand guard over the Constitution itself, immune (in theory) from political winds.

Together, this architecture formed a bulwark against tyranny — a system so intricate and deliberate that no single faction could control it without the consent of many others.

But that system no longer exists as it was intended.

THE RISE OF THE MANAGERIAL STATE ——————

Today, unelected bureaucrats write regulations with the force of law. Corporate lobbyists craft legislation and fund the campaigns of those who vote on it. State governments are little more than administrative arms of the federal leviathan, bound by mandates and choked by matching fund schemes.

We've replaced **representation with influence, citizen governance with consultant class manipulation,** and **federalism with forced compliance.** The republic was designed to work slowly, deliberately, and with caution. Now it lurches forward at the whim of donors, data firms, and media consultants — driven not by civic will, but by polling and profit.

This is not dysfunction. It is **systemic corruption** disguised as governance.

We are told the political system is broken. In reality, it has been **repurposed** — no longer designed to serve the people, but to manage them. No longer constructed to defend liberty, but to **administer compliance**.

The Constitution has not failed. We have simply abandoned its structure.

MODERN DYSFUNCTION: A SYMPTOM, NOT A CAUSE

Political polarization, legislative gridlock, and public distrust are not the disease — they are **symptoms of a deeper failure**. That failure is structural.

We can trace the breakdown of our republic through specific inflection points:

- **1913**: The **17th Amendment** stripped state legislatures of their power to elect U.S. Senators, severing the last direct link between the federal government and the sovereign states. In that same year, the **Federal Reserve Act** created a central banking system controlled not by Congress, but by private banks. And the **16th Amendment** gave the federal government a direct pipeline to the income of every citizen, bypassing state intermediaries.

- **1970s–2000s:** The rise of **political action committees (PACs)** and **dark money organizations** blurred the lines between speech and spending. Campaigns became marketing machines — fueled by data, driven by cash, and designed to win, not represent.

- **2010:** The **Citizens United** decision turned campaign finance law on its head. Corporations and special interests were now granted full political speech rights — not as people, but as perpetual, profit-driven entities. This ruling didn't create corruption; it legalized it.

Each of these milestones — sold as "modernization" or "progress" — was in fact a **deliberate step away from Madisonian balance and toward elite consolidation**.

A FORK IN THE ROAD

This book is not about nostalgia. It is about **truth**. We are no longer governed by the system our ancestors fought to establish. We are governed by a system that **mimics its forms but subverts its function**.

The Senate still exists, but it no longer represents the states.

Elections are still held, but their outcomes are sculpted by money and media.

Laws are still passed, but they are ghostwritten by those who will profit from them.

The structure of the republic has been hollowed out and replaced with a managerial elite who answer not to the people — but to donors, data, and interests that operate far outside public view.

But the Constitution still stands. The principles still exist. And the torch of liberty — though dimmed — has not been extinguished.

In the chapters that follow, we will trace **exactly how we lost the republic**, and more importantly, **how we can begin to restore it**.

This is not a partisan call. It is a **constitutional one**. It is not about left or right — it is about the vertical balance of power that once protected liberty and now empowers control.

If we are to reclaim the vision of a free people in a self-governing republic, we must understand what was taken, how it was done, and who benefits from keeping it that way.

Only then can we chart a course back.

CHAPTER 1

The Founders' Vision of Balance

"Ambition must be made to counteract ambition."

— James Madison, *Federalist No. 51*

When the Founders sat down to design the government of the United States, they were not inventing a democracy. They were engineering a **balance of forces** — a political structure whose primary purpose was not speed, not simplicity, but **stability** through **opposition**.

The framers of the Constitution understood something modern America has largely forgotten: that **power must be constrained not only by law, but by structure**. Laws can be repealed. Elections can be manipulated. But a well-designed system — one that pits interest against interest, level against level — is much harder to subvert.

The genius of the American experiment was not just its commitment to liberty, but its **architecture of resistance** — a compound republic in which power was distributed, diluted, and disputed by design.

And nowhere was that design more critical than in the original construction of the **United States Senate**.

THE SENATE: NOT A MIRROR OF THE PEOPLE, BUT A GUARDIAN OF THE STATES

In today's political imagination, both houses of Congress are assumed to represent the people. But under the Constitution as originally written, this was only **half true**.

The **House of Representatives** was intended to represent **the people** — elected directly by popular vote, proportionally based on population. It was designed to reflect the passions, opinions, and interests of ordinary citizens — and to change rapidly as public sentiment shifted.

But the **Senate** was something entirely different. Under **Article I, Section 3** of the Constitution, **U.S. Senators were chosen by the legislatures of each state**, not by the people directly. The Senate existed not to reflect popular will, but to **represent the sovereign interests of the states** themselves.

Each state, regardless of size or population, was given **two senators** — a deliberate structural equality that served as a counterweight to the majoritarian impulses of the House. This wasn't just a compromise between large and small states; it was a **guardrail against federal centralization**.

The purpose was explicit: the states were not subdivisions of the federal government. They were coequal parties to the constitutional compact. And the Senate was their formal presence within the machinery of federal power.

In this design, the people had a voice (the House), but the states had a **seat at the table** (the Senate).

FEDERALISM IN PRACTICE: A SYSTEM OF INTERNAL TENSION

The Founders designed a **federal republic**, not a national democracy. The distinction is critical.

Under a federal system:

- **The federal government** manages national and international affairs.
- **The states** retain authority over most domestic and civil matters.
- **The people**, through both federal and state systems, maintain sovereignty — but filtered through **distinct channels of representation**.

This wasn't an accident — it was an intentional effort to prevent any one faction from capturing the whole system.

Each level of government — local, state, and federal — was designed to **check the others**. This multilayered structure served as a brake on runaway legislation, centralized power, and populist demagoguery.

Madison described this system as "a double security... to the rights of the people." (*Federalist No. 51*)

In a national democracy, everything flows from a single source — the majority. But in a compound republic, **sovereignty is fragmented**. Legislation must survive scrutiny from **multiple constituencies**, each with its own interests and mechanisms of control.

This is why the original method of senatorial selection was so crucial. By having **state legislatures choose U.S. Senators**, the Constitution gave **the states institutional power within the federal system** — not just influence, but actual representation.

It meant that any major shift in federal authority required **alignment between the people and the states**, not just a simple majority vote.

REPRESENTATION VS. POPULAR WILL —————

Modern political discourse assumes that more democracy equals more freedom. But the Founders understood that **unchecked popular will** is just another form of tyranny — one with a smiling face and a fleeting attention span.

True representation, in their view, was not about immediate reflection of public opinion. It was about **filtered consent** — the idea that decisions should be made by those chosen for their judgment, not merely their popularity.

This is why the Constitution placed so many **deliberate buffers** between raw public opinion and the machinery of governance:

- The **Electoral College** buffered the presidency from direct popular election.
- The **Senate**, as originally conceived, insulated legislation from populist swings.
- **Lifetime judicial appointments** shielded the courts from electoral politics.
- The concept of **enumerated powers** limited what the federal government could do at all.

These were not barriers to democracy. They were **bulwarks for liberty** — designed to slow the passions of the moment and force deliberation, compromise, and restraint.

In this context, **the popular election of senators** was not progress. It was a dismantling of the very safeguards meant to preserve the republic.

WARNINGS FROM THE FOUNDERS ————————

The Founders were not naïve idealists. They understood that power, once unchained, seeks only to expand. They had seen it in monarchies, in parliaments, and in revolutions gone awry. That's why they wrote not just for the moment, but for **eternity**.

Many of the core warnings against consolidating power into a single channel came from the Constitution's authors themselves.

- **James Madison**, the "Father of the Constitution," warned repeatedly that democracy without checks becomes a tyranny of the majority. In *Federalist No. 10*, he argued that the structure of the republic must "refine and enlarge the public views" through **indirect representation**.
- **Alexander Hamilton**, in *Federalist No. 9*, emphasized that "a firm union will be of the utmost moment to the peace and liberty of the states," but only if it preserved the independence and authority of each level of government.
- **George Washington**, in his Farewell Address, cautioned against "the spirit of party," and the danger of centralized political control masquerading as national unity.
- **Thomas Jefferson**, though more democratic in instinct, nonetheless feared a federal government that grew beyond its constitutional boundaries. "The natural progress of things," he wrote, "is for liberty to yield, and government to gain ground."

These were not abstractions. These were road signs — **explicit warnings against the very centralization we now see as normal**.

THE COST OF IGNORING THE DESIGN ————————

The 17th Amendment, which we'll examine in detail in the next chapter, did not simply change how senators are elected. It **severed the last direct link between the federal government and the states**.

With that single change, the Senate became **redundant with the House** — another body elected by the people, subject to the same donor pressures, media cycles, and party machinery. The states were reduced from partners in the constitutional compact to **subordinates of federal authority**.

The result has been exactly what Madison, Hamilton, and Jefferson feared: a slow-motion collapse of federalism, the rise of administrative control, and a population increasingly alienated from the institutions that claim to represent them.

This book is not a lament for the past. It is a warning for the present — and a blueprint for the future.

If we are to reclaim the liberties our ancestors fought for, we must first understand the **mechanism they built to preserve them**.

That mechanism was balance.
It was resistance.
It was federalism.
And we have lost it.

CHAPTER 2

The Rise of Direct Democracy
– The 17th Amendment

*"Democracy never lasts long. It soon wastes, exhausts,
and murders itself."*

— John Adams

The 17th Amendment is widely praised as a democratic reform —
a correction to an outdated process and a triumph for the people
over corrupt elites. This is how it is taught in schools, spoken of in
politics, and enshrined in modern American mythology.

But the reality is far more sobering.

The 17th Amendment did not empower the people. It **disempowered
the states**. It did not eliminate corruption — it merely changed its
location. And it did not make the system more representative — it
hollowed out a key pillar of federalism, turning the Senate from

a deliberative voice of state governments into a redundant echo chamber of national populism.

This chapter explores the **origin, political pressure, and unintended consequences** of the 17th Amendment — and how its passage marked the beginning of the end of the **compound republic** the Founders designed.

PROGRESSIVE REFORM OR POLITICAL POWER PLAY?

The early 20th century was a time of immense change in the United States. Industrialization had transformed the economy, immigration had reshaped cities, and the Gilded Age had exposed levels of wealth disparity and corporate influence never seen before.

The **Progressive Era** — roughly 1890 to 1920 — emerged as a national response to these pressures. Reformers called for antitrust laws, labor protections, voting rights for women, and campaign finance oversight. At its best, the movement sought to **curb elite power and restore dignity to the common citizen**.

But like most political movements, progressivism was not monolithic. Beneath its surface were **factions with competing agendas**, and not all reforms shared the same constitutional integrity. Among the most aggressive reforms was the push for **direct election of U.S. Senators** — a cause championed by populists and Progressive politicians who viewed the Senate as **corrupt, elitist, and anti-democratic**.

Their solution? Remove the middlemen — state legislatures — and put the power directly in the hands of voters.

What was framed as a blow to corruption was, in truth, a **fundamental redefinition of the American constitutional structure**.

POPULIST PRESSURE VS. STRUCTURAL CONSEQUENCES

The demand for direct election of senators had been building for decades, with early advocates arguing that state legislatures were too easily influenced or deadlocked by special interests. Indeed, some states had failed to appoint senators for months or even years due to political stalemates.

But these cases were **exceptions**, not the rule. And the solution — direct election — was akin to amputating a limb to treat a sprain.

The Founders never intended for the Senate to be democratic in the popular sense. Its very purpose was to **slow down democracy**, to add a layer of insulation between momentary passions and long-term national policy. The state legislatures acted as a filter — selecting senators who reflected not the whims of the populace, but the strategic interests of the states themselves.

When that filter was removed, the Senate ceased to be a voice for the states. It became a **second House of Representatives**, elected by the same constituency, influenced by the same money, and driven by the same short-term electoral incentives.

This was the **structural consequence** of populist pressure: the slow but certain death of vertical representation — the idea that both people and states have a role in national governance.

THE CORRUPTION NARRATIVE: CONVENIENT, BUT INCOMPLETE

Proponents of the 17th Amendment argued that the old system was **rife with bribery and backroom deals**. And to a degree, they were right. There were high-profile cases — such as William Clark of Montana, who allegedly bought his way into the Senate in the 1890s — that provided ample fodder for reformers.

But here's the critical point: **corruption existed not because of the system, but because of the human element within it**. Corruption was not exclusive to state legislatures. It simply occurred there because that was the point of selection.

After the 17th Amendment, corruption did not disappear. It **migrated** — into party primaries, national fundraising machines, and centralized media platforms. The influence of money in politics grew, not shrank, because it was no longer constrained by **local accountability**.

In fact, one could argue the modern system is **far more corrupt**, albeit in more sophisticated ways. Senators now raise millions from out-of-state donors, cater to national parties, and owe their political lives to corporate PACs and Super PACs rather than to the states they claim to represent.

What changed wasn't the morality of politicians. It was the **structure that once limited their ambitions**.

WHAT THE 17TH AMENDMENT ACTUALLY SAYS

The full text of the 17th Amendment is short, but its impact is profound:

"The Senate of the United States shall be composed of two Senators from each State, elected by the people thereof…"

With this single sentence, **state legislatures were stripped of one of their primary roles in the federal system**.

To the average citizen, this may seem like a win for democracy. But in constitutional terms, it was a **shift in sovereignty**.

Under the original system:

- The **House** represented the people.
- The **Senate** represented the states.
- The **President** was indirectly elected by electors chosen by the states.
- The **Supreme Court** interpreted the boundaries between them.

After the 17th Amendment:

- The Senate no longer represented the states.
- The balance of power tilted permanently in favor of federal centralization.

This was not just a procedural change. It was a **seismic realignment of constitutional purpose**.

COLLAPSE OF STATE SOVEREIGNTY

When states lost their voice in the Senate, they lost their ability to block or negotiate federal encroachments. Over the ensuing decades, Congress passed sweeping legislation that would have once been **resisted by state-appointed senators**:

- Massive federal grant programs with strings attached
- Nationwide education and healthcare mandates
- Expansions of federal criminal law and regulation
- Interventions into state infrastructure and labor policy

Why didn't the Senate stop these overreaches? Because by then, **senators no longer represented the states. They represented themselves — and the wealthy elite voters and donors who kept them in power.**

This transformation explains why **modern federalism is a shadow of its former self**. The states still exist, but they are **administrative zones**, not sovereign partners. They comply with federal regulations not because they agree — but because they are **financially coerced** through matching funds, conditional grants, and threatened loss of revenue.

Had the 17th Amendment never passed, the explosion of federal authority in the 20th century would have encountered **institutional resistance** from a Senate loyal to the states. Instead, that resistance was quietly dismantled.

A SENATE REIMAGINED: THEN AND NOW

To grasp the scale of this transformation, consider how different the Senate looked before 1913:

Before the 17th Amendment

- Senators were appointed by state legislatures.
- They could be recalled or replaced based on state interests.
- Campaign fundraising was minimal.
- Senators often had deep experience in state law and governance.
- The Senate served as a buffer between federal ambition and state autonomy.

After the 17th Amendment

- Senators are elected by popular vote.
- They campaign for months and raise millions from national sources.

- Loyalty often lies with party leaders and national interest groups.
- The incentive is to serve **the majority**, not the state.
- The Senate mirrors the House in both behavior and structure.

SENATE REPRESENTATION BEFORE AND AFTER THE 17TH AMENDMENT

Pre-17th Amendment	Post-17th Amendment
Selected by state legislatures	Elected by popular vote
Represented state governments	Represents the people directly
Accountable to state interests	Accountable to donors and party
Check on federal expansion	Often rubber-stamp for federal power
Slower, deliberate governance	Faster, partisan-aligned action

THE IRONY OF "MORE DEMOCRATIC"

Supporters of the 17th Amendment argued that **more democracy equals more legitimacy**. But in practice, **removing state legislatures from the Senate selection process weakened accountability, not strengthened it.**

State legislatures are **more accessible** to average citizens than national campaigns. Local voters have more influence over their state senators than over a U.S. Senate race dominated by national media and outside money.

By inserting direct election into the Senate, we didn't make it more democratic. We made it **more detached from the people it was designed to serve**.

This is the paradox of progressivism: In trying to eliminate corruption and give power to the people, it often creates **systems too large, too distant, and too manipulated for the people to control**.

WHAT WE LOST — AND WHY IT MATTERS NOW

The 17th Amendment was not a single misstep. It was the first major **institutional break** in the framework the Founders built. It signaled that structure no longer mattered — that function would be sacrificed for sentiment.

And once one structural safeguard was removed, others followed:

- The rise of permanent political parties
- The centralization of campaign finance
- The growth of the federal administrative state
- Judicial reinterpretation of enumerated powers

These are not random developments. They are **logical outcomes of a system no longer bound by its original architecture**.

If we hope to restore balance, we must recognize the 17th Amendment as the **constitutional turning point** it truly was.

CONCLUSION: A CAUTIONARY REFORM —————

Not all reform is progress. Not all change is improvement. The 17th Amendment stands as a **cautionary tale** of what happens when **we prioritize emotional appeals over structural design**.

It is easy to be swept up in the rhetoric of "giving power to the people." But in governance, **form matters**. Structure matters. And when you dismantle the mechanisms that prevent tyranny, you will — in time — be ruled by it.

In the next chapter, we will examine how another major shift in 1913 — the creation of the **Federal Reserve and the federal income tax** — laid the foundation for elite financial control of the republic, completing the political transformation the 17th Amendment had begun.

Senate Representation Before and After the 17th Amendment

Feature	Pre-17th Amendment	Pre-17th Amendment
Selection Method	Selected by state legislatures	Elected by popular vote
Primary Representation	Represented state governments	Represents the people directly
Accountability	Accountable to state interests	Accountable to donors and party
Function	Check on federal expansion	Rubber-stamp for federal power
Governing Style	Deliberate governance	Partisan-aligned action

CHAPTER 3

The Federal Reserve & the Income Tax – 1913's Trojan Horse

"Give me control of a nation's money supply, and I care not who makes its laws."

— Mayer Amschel Rothschild (attributed)

In the year 1913, the architecture of the American republic was quietly, fundamentally altered — not by war or rebellion, but by legislation and amendments presented as progress. Three seismic shifts occurred:

- The **16th Amendment** established the federal income tax.
- The **17th Amendment** removed state control over the Senate.
- The **Federal Reserve Act** created a centralized banking authority.

Individually, each change might be explained away as necessary reform. Together, they represent a **coordinated redirection of power** — away from the states, away from the people, and toward a **centralized administrative-financial elite**. It was, in effect, **the Trojan Horse of the 20th century**: a transformation cloaked in reformist language, delivered through legal process, but devastating to constitutional balance.

FINANCIAL CENTRALIZATION AND POLITICAL REALIGNMENT

To understand the full implications of 1913, we must view these events not in isolation, but in sequence.

The Founders had created a government with carefully restrained taxing power and strictly limited banking functions. The Constitution allowed Congress to **collect duties, imposts, and excises**, but it explicitly forbade **direct taxes unless apportioned by population**. This was meant to prevent the federal government from having the means to dominate the economy or burden individual citizens without direct accountability.

Similarly, the U.S. government had no central bank. The idea of a **national bank** had been contentious since the days of Hamilton and Jefferson, and previous attempts — like the First and Second Banks of the United States — had expired amid fierce debate about overreach and cronyism.

But by the early 1900s, powerful financial interests — industrialists, Wall Street bankers, and international lenders — were pressing for a unified currency, centralized credit, and more predictable mechanisms for government borrowing.

Their opportunity came with the crises of the day: economic panics, industrial consolidation, and the rising tide of Progressivism. Reformers wanted more equity. Bankers wanted more control. And political leaders wanted more revenue.

In 1913, they all got what they wanted. But **the people and the states got less than they bargained for**.

THE 16TH AMENDMENT: A NEW KIND OF TAXATION

"The power to tax involves the power to destroy."

— Chief Justice John Marshall

Prior to 1913, the federal government **relied on tariffs and excise taxes** for most of its revenue. These taxes were broad-based, indirect, and naturally limited in scope. While imperfect, this system constrained the size and ambition of the federal government because it **constrained its funding**.

The **16th Amendment** changed everything.

"The Congress shall have power to lay and collect taxes on incomes, from whatever source derived, without apportionment among the several States..."

This removed the constitutional requirement that **direct taxes be apportioned by population** — a vital check that had prevented disproportionate federal targeting of individuals or industries.

Now, the federal government could tax personal income **without regard to state populations or representation**. This had profound implications:

- **The states were bypassed** entirely in the process of revenue generation.
- **The federal government became dependent on individual taxpayers**, not the states.
- **Redistributive taxation** — once nearly impossible — became the norm.

At first, the income tax was modest, affecting only the wealthiest Americans. But like most "temporary" taxes, it became permanent, normalized, and increasingly expansive.

As the decades progressed, the tax code was weaponized — used to reward favored constituencies, punish disfavored behaviors, and manipulate the economy. Congress discovered that through taxation, it could control not just revenue, but **personal behavior, industry, and even thought**.

THE FEDERAL RESERVE ACT: PRIVATIZING THE MONEY POWER

If the income tax gave the government **access to the people's wealth**, the **Federal Reserve Act** gave elite bankers **control over its creation and distribution**.

Passed just months after the 16th and 17th Amendments, the **Federal Reserve Act of 1913** established a quasi-private central bank with the authority to:

- Issue currency (Federal Reserve Notes)
- Set interest rates and banking reserve requirements
- Regulate credit and liquidity
- Act as a lender of last resort

While technically overseen by Congress, the Federal Reserve was **intentionally insulated from democratic control**. Its decisions were made by a board of unelected governors and regional banks, with heavy influence from private financial institutions.

This was not a government agency in the traditional sense. It was a **public-private hybrid**, designed to **serve the needs of the financial system**, not the public.

And it worked — just not for everyone.

- Wall Street gained stability.
- The federal government gained borrowing power.

- The people gained inflation, debt, and dependence.

Through monetary policy, the Fed could now **inflate or deflate the economy**, engineer booms and busts, and redirect the flow of credit toward favored sectors. Congress, freed from the need to balance budgets, began passing **unfunded mandates** and authorizing debt with little concern for long-term consequences.

Over time, the Fed became **the most powerful unelected institution in the country** — and arguably, the least understood.

THE HIDDEN ALIGNMENT OF 1913

It's no coincidence that all three pillars of 1913's transformation — income tax, Federal Reserve, and direct election of senators — **mutually reinforced each other**.

- The **16th Amendment** gave Washington the money.
- The **Federal Reserve** gave it the borrowing capacity.
- The **17th Amendment** eliminated state resistance to federal overreach.

Together, they formed a closed system in which:

- The government could tax its citizens directly.
- It could borrow nearly unlimited amounts through central banking.

- It no longer needed state governments as partners — only as clients.

This was not merely a shift in policy. It was a shift in **sovereignty**.

The compound republic became a centralized bureaucracy. The states became subordinates. And the people became **instruments of revenue** — not masters of their own governance.

THE 1913 REALIGNMENT

Year	Event	Impact
Feb 3	**16th Amendment Ratified**	Federal power to tax individuals directly
April	**First Income Tax Implemented**	Top rate of 7% on wealthy earners
May 31	**17th Amendment Ratified**	Direct election of senators
Dec 23	**Federal Reserve Act Signed**	Central bank created, dollar control shifted

THE MYTH OF REFORM: WHO REALLY BENEFITED?

Progressives believed they were taming capitalism and empowering the people. In reality, **the changes of 1913 concentrated power more than any single moment in American peacetime history.**

Who benefited?

- **Bankers**, who now had a protected institution ensuring liquidity and minimizing risk.
- **Federal politicians**, who could now tax and borrow without consent from state governments.
- **National parties**, who gained uniform control over the Senate through nationalized elections.
- **Corporate interests**, who quickly learned to manipulate monetary policy, tax codes, and campaign finance systems to their advantage.

Meanwhile, the American citizen became:

- A taxpayer with fewer local protections
- A voter increasingly irrelevant in national outcomes
- A debtor through inflation and national borrowing

THE RIPPLE EFFECT INTO THE 20TH CENTURY ——

With the power to tax, borrow, and print money consolidated, the federal government grew exponentially:

- **New Deal programs**, World Wars, and social spending were all funded by the new system.
- **Debt ceilings** were raised year after year, often without resistance.
- **Dollar devaluation** became an accepted economic policy.

- **Inflation**, once rare and temporary, became a permanent fixture.

And with each expansion, the average citizen became **less sovereign, less secure, and more dependent**.

CONCLUSION: A TROJAN HORSE DELIVERED IN BROAD DAYLIGHT

1913 was not a coup. It was a **revolution wrapped in legality**.

Each step — the income tax, the Federal Reserve, the direct election of senators — was passed through formal channels. But each step also **undermined the structural constraints** the Constitution had imposed on centralized power.

These changes were not inevitable. They were orchestrated. And their consequences continue to define American governance to this day.

Understanding the events of 1913 is not optional — it is **essential** for anyone who seeks to restore balance to our republic. Because without reversing or restraining the mechanisms unleashed that year, any talk of reform will be **superficial at best**.

In the next chapter, we will trace how the concentration of money and power — accelerated by 1913 — gave rise to **PACs, Super PACs, and the privatization of political influence**. If 1913 laid the foundation, **the campaign finance explosion completed the structure**.

1913: The Year the Balance of Power Was Broken

Date	Event	Impact
Feb 3, 1913	16th Amendment Ratified	Federal power to tax individuals directly
April 1913	First Federal Income Tax Implemented	Initial 1-7% income tax on top earners
May 31, 1913	17th Amendment Ratified	Senators elected by popular vote instead of state legislatures
Dec 23, 1913	Federal Reserve Act Signed	Central bank established; monetary control shifted from Congress

CHAPTER 4

PACs, Super PACs, and the Privatization of Power

"Representative government assumes that the people have access to the facts."

— Daniel Patrick Moynihan

The Constitution made no mention of political parties, corporations, or billion-dollar campaigns. The Founders envisioned a system where citizens chose local leaders to represent their interests in distant halls of power — not a system where **private money manipulates public outcomes** through a web of influence and messaging.

But over time, as legal loopholes widened and elections became nationalized media spectacles, political influence became a **commodity** — traded, concentrated, and weaponized by the few who could afford to dominate the narrative.

This chapter traces how America transitioned from a republic of voters to a **plutocracy of funders**, beginning long before Citizens United and culminating in the rise of **PACs, Super PACs, and the legalized auction of government**.

CAMPAIGN FINANCE BEFORE CITIZENS UNITED

To understand the present, we must examine the evolution of campaign finance regulation — and its systematic unraveling.

Before the 1970s, campaign finance was largely unregulated. Corporations, unions, and wealthy individuals could funnel funds to candidates with few restrictions. Corruption was rampant, often hidden in the shadows of handshake deals and party machines.

The first major attempt to impose order came with the **Federal Election Campaign Act (FECA) of 1971**, later amended in 1974 after Watergate. FECA:

- Created the **Federal Election Commission (FEC)**
- Imposed **limits on individual and PAC contributions**
- Mandated disclosure of donations
- Provided **public financing** for presidential candidates

These reforms were intended to restore faith in the electoral process. But they also triggered a counter-effort — not to comply, but to **circumvent**.

The first wave of legal creativity gave rise to **Political Action Committees (PACs)** — organizations that could collect contributions and donate to candidates within regulated limits. PACs were often affiliated with unions, corporations, or ideological groups. But it didn't stop there.

THE RISE OF PACS AND 527 ORGANIZATIONS ———

In the 1980s and 1990s, lawyers and operatives discovered that the system left gaping holes:

- **Soft money** — unregulated contributions to parties for "party-building activities"
- **Issue advocacy** — ads that didn't use the "magic words" ("vote for," "elect," "defeat") could be funded without limits

This gave rise to **527 organizations** — named after a section of the IRS code — which could raise unlimited funds as long as they didn't coordinate directly with candidates.

By the early 2000s, campaign finance had become a chessboard:

- Candidates raised **hard money** under strict limits.
- Parties raised **soft money** with looser rules.
- Outside groups (527s, later 501(c)4s) spent millions on **"independent" issue ads** that were, in truth, **thinly veiled campaign efforts**.

The 2002 **Bipartisan Campaign Reform Act (McCain-Feingold)** sought to shut down soft money and limit coordination. But the law quickly ran into **constitutional challenges**, and enforcement was weak.

Rather than contain the influence of money, McCain-Feingold **drove it further underground** — setting the stage for the legal explosion to come.

CITIZENS UNITED: THE FLOODGATES OPEN

In 2010, the Supreme Court issued its ruling in **Citizens United v. FEC**, declaring that **corporations and unions have First Amendment rights to engage in unlimited independent political spending**.

The majority reasoned that "independent expenditures do not give rise to corruption" and that the identity of the speaker — whether a person or a corporation — was irrelevant to free speech protections.

The result?

- Corporations, unions, and billionaires could spend unlimited money to support or oppose candidates — as long as it wasn't coordinated with a campaign.
- Super PACs (independent expenditure-only committees) could now raise and spend **unlimited funds** from individuals, corporations, and unions.

Citizens United didn't invent money in politics. It **unleashed it**. What had been a trickle of circumvention became a **torrent of influence** — flooding congressional races, judicial campaigns, ballot initiatives, and presidential elections.

Suddenly, political power was no longer a function of representation — it was a function of **fundraising capacity and donor loyalty**.

THE INFLUENCE WEB: MEDIA, DONORS, AND MESSAGING

In a post–Citizens United landscape, the **influence ecosystem** looks like this:

1. **Donors** (billionaires, corporations, unions) contribute unlimited funds to Super PACs and dark money nonprofits.
2. **Consultants and strategists** funnel that money into ad buys, social media campaigns, and voter data operations.
3. **Media outlets**, saturated with campaign ad revenue, grow dependent on election cycles and avoid alienating advertisers.
4. **Candidates**, desperate to keep up, tailor their platforms to donor interests — or risk being primaried, smeared, or ignored.
5. **Voters**, overwhelmed by messaging, often choose based on brand recognition, fear-based appeals, or media spin — not policy.

The result? A self-reinforcing machine in which:

- Access to capital determines political viability
- Message saturation outweighs deliberation
- True grassroots candidates are priced out or drowned out
- Policy decisions are shaped in boardrooms, not town halls

This is **privatized power** — the transformation of political influence from a **civic process into a commercial product**.

CASE STUDIES OF DISTORTION: KOCH NETWORK AND SOROS SPENDING

To illustrate the scale of this transformation, we turn to two of the most influential players on opposite ends of the political spectrum.

The Koch Network

Charles and the late David Koch, heirs to a vast oil and energy empire, built a **political infrastructure rivaling that of major parties**. Their network:

- Funded dozens of libertarian think tanks, advocacy groups, and Super PACs
- Spent hundreds of millions on state and federal elections
- Created the **Americans for Prosperity** brand to push free-market policies
- Built data operations to rival national committees

Through this network, the Kochs influenced:

- Tax policy
- Environmental regulation
- Education reform
- Judicial nominations

Importantly, most of their influence was not through candidate donations, but through **issue advocacy**, think tanks, and media pipelines — all **legal under current campaign finance law**.

George Soros and Open Society

On the left, billionaire George Soros has used his **Open Society Foundations** and a constellation of 501(c)(3) and (c)(4) organizations to:

- Fund voter mobilization
- Shape media narratives
- Influence local district attorney races
- Support liberal judicial and immigration reforms

Soros doesn't act through the Democratic Party per se — he funds **parallel institutions** that apply pressure from the outside.

In both cases, the donor is not acting illegally. They are **maximizing influence within the legal framework**, using **money, message, and media** to achieve ideological goals.

But the outcome is the same: **policy shaped by wealth, not representation**.

PAC & Super PAC Influence Flowchart

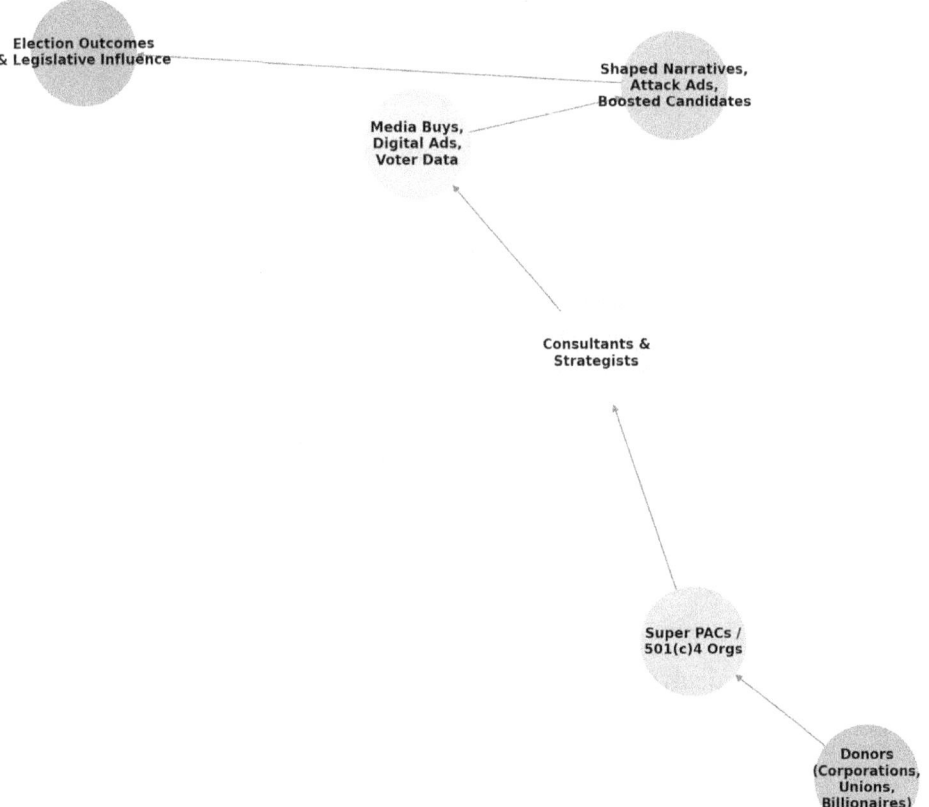

- **Top Tier: Donors** (corporations, unions, individuals)
- → Fund Super PACs, 501(c)4s
- → Hire Consultants & Strategists
- → Media Buys / Digital Ads / Voter Targeting
- → Shaping Narratives, Attacking Opponents, Boosting Candidates
- → Outcome: Electoral victories & legislative influence

THE EFFECTS ON REPRESENTATION ────────

When campaign finance is dominated by outside money, several things happen:

- **Incumbents become dependent** on their donor network, not their district.
- **Challengers must appeal to national donors**, often distorting local issues.
- **Elected officials avoid controversial votes**, fearing donor backlash.
- **State and local autonomy declines**, as national money dictates local outcomes.

This undermines the very **Madisonian balance** the Constitution sought to preserve. The problem is not that money talks — it's that **money has drowned out everyone else**.

THE ILLUSION OF INDEPENDENCE ────────

Supporters of Citizens United argue that "independent expenditures" can't corrupt candidates. But in practice:

- Candidates know who is funding the ads
- Donors know what the candidate supports
- Coordination occurs through public messaging, shared consultants, and aligned agendas

True independence is a fiction.

The result is a political class that is **responsive to interests, not constituents** — and a system where ideas rise or fall **not on merit, but on marketing**.

CONCLUSION: THE SALE OF THE REPUBLIC ——

PACs and Super PACs did not kill democracy. But they **privatized it** — turning the republic into a pay-to-play arena where influence is auctioned, not earned.

The Founders feared monarchy, but they could not have imagined a world where power is neither inherited nor elected — but **purchased**.

Until we address the influence of money in politics — not just through law, but through structural reform — we will remain trapped in a system where **elections are won by wealth, not will**.

In the next chapter, we examine how the **Citizens United ruling** institutionalized this transformation — and why overturning it is not enough unless we also restore the constitutional balance beneath it.

CHAPTER 5

Citizens United and the Final Shift

"The Court's ruling threatens to undermine the integrity of elected institutions across the Nation."

— Justice John Paul Stevens, dissent
in *Citizens United v. FEC* (2010)

"The premise of our Bill of Rights is that the government may not prohibit speech because it disagrees with the speaker's identity or message."

— Justice Antonin Scalia, concurring opinion

The **Citizens United v. Federal Election Commission** decision in 2010 did not invent money in politics — but it fundamentally changed the relationship between **money, speech, and power** in the American system.

To fully understand why Citizens United is considered by many the final rupture in the balance of representative government, we must dissect not only the ruling itself, but the assumptions that underlie it — and the implications it has had for every level of American political life since.

THE CASE THAT CHANGED EVERYTHING

The case originated from a conservative nonprofit organization, **Citizens United**, which sought to air and promote a film critical of Hillary Clinton during the 2008 Democratic primaries. The film, *Hillary: The Movie*, was considered by the FEC to be **electioneering communication** — essentially, a campaign ad that fell under restrictions imposed by the **Bipartisan Campaign Reform Act (BCRA)**, commonly known as **McCain-Feingold**.

Citizens United sued, arguing that the government could not constitutionally restrict the group from airing the film because it constituted **political speech** protected by the First Amendment.

What began as a relatively narrow question — whether one nonprofit could fund a specific political film — evolved into a sweeping reconsideration of whether **corporations and unions could be barred from spending money independently to support or oppose candidates at all**.

On **January 21, 2010**, in a 5–4 decision, the Supreme Court ruled in favor of Citizens United, striking down **Section 203 of the BCRA** and holding that:

- **Corporations and unions have a First Amendment right** to engage in independent political expenditures
- The government may **not suppress political speech based on the speaker's corporate identity**
- Independent expenditures (as opposed to direct contributions) do **not lead to quid pro quo corruption**

The decision immediately removed barriers that had prevented corporations and unions from using their general treasury funds to produce ads and messaging advocating the election or defeat of specific candidates.

The majority opinion, written by **Justice Anthony Kennedy**, concluded:

"Political speech is indispensable to a democracy, which is no less true because the speech comes from a corporation."

THE DISSENT: A WARNING IGNORED

The dissent, written by **Justice John Paul Stevens**, delivered a searing rebuke. Stevens, joined by Justices Ginsburg, Breyer, and Sotomayor, warned that:

- The ruling gave **"unprecedented" political power to corporations**, entities that are not citizens and do not vote.
- It would result in **massive distortions** in the democratic process by allowing wealth to drown out the voices of individuals.
- The notion that independent expenditures are non-corrupting was **naïve and ahistorical**.

Stevens argued:

"The Court's ruling threatens to undermine the integrity of elected institutions across the Nation. It is a rejection of the common sense of the American people."

He emphasized that corporations are not natural persons — they are **legal constructs**, created by the state, with privileges but without the same duties or moral conscience as human beings. To grant them the same political rights as individuals was to **redefine citizenship itself**.

THE NEW DEFINITION OF SPEECH ─────────────

At the heart of Citizens United lies a pivotal philosophical question:
Is money speech?
And if so, does limiting political spending equate to **censorship**?

The Court answered yes — not just in theory, but in practice. In doing so, it **blurred the line between expression and influence**.

While it's true that producing a political ad or film requires money, the ruling extended **constitutional protection not just to the act of speaking**, but to the **act of spending** — regardless of the source.

This redefinition had immediate consequences:

- It created **a dual class of political actors**: those with capital to spend freely, and those without it.
- It gave corporations, unions, and extremely wealthy individuals **direct tools to shape public discourse** in ways the average citizen could not match.
- It eroded the concept of **equal political voice**, a pillar of representative democracy.

In theory, speech remained free. In practice, it became **proportional to wealth**.

SUPER PACS: THE ENGINE OF INFLUENCE ———

Though Citizens United did not directly create **Super PACs**, it laid the groundwork for them.

Shortly after the ruling, a federal appeals court in *SpeechNow.org v. FEC* ruled that **if independent expenditures could not be limited, then the groups that made them could also raise unlimited funds**.

This led to the creation of **independent expenditure-only committees** — now known as **Super PACs**.

Super PACs can:

- Raise unlimited sums from corporations, unions, and individuals
- Spend unlimited sums advocating for or against candidates
- Avoid contribution caps and often hide donor sources via 501(c)(4) "dark money" groups

The only requirement is that they remain "independent" — that is, they **cannot coordinate directly** with candidates or campaigns.

But in reality, "coordination" is easy to avoid. Candidates and Super PACs can:

- Use **public messaging to signal intent**
- Share consultants, vendors, or legal teams
- Promote aligned narratives and issue agendas

The line between campaign and PAC has become **effectively meaningless**.

IMPACT ON STATE AND FEDERAL ELECTIONS ─

The effects of Citizens United and Super PACs have been felt **at every level of American government**:

- In federal elections, Super PACs now spend **more than political parties in many key races**

- In state elections, outside money often **drowns out local voices**, allowing national donors to reshape local agendas
- In judicial races — especially for state supreme courts — Super PAC funding has led to the **politicization of the judiciary**, with massive outside expenditures swaying nonpartisan contests

This has created a perverse cycle:

1. Candidates raise money to survive primaries.
2. Super PACs step in with attack ads and narrative control.
3. Voters are bombarded with messaging designed not to inform, but to incite.
4. Elected officials enter office already **beholden to donors**, not voters.

And because Super PACs are protected by Citizens United, they are **effectively untouchable** by most campaign finance laws.

THE ILLUSION OF INDEPENDENCE

Supporters of *Citizens United* argue that "independent expenditures" can't corrupt candidates. But in practice:

- Candidates know who is funding the ads
- Donors know what the candidate supports
- Coordination occurs through public messaging, shared consultants, and aligned agendas

True independence is a fiction.

The result is a political class that is **responsive to interests, not constituents** — and a system where ideas rise or fall **not on merit, but on marketing**.

A REVEALING ADMISSION FROM THE INSIDE ——

No critique of the current system is more damning than the one made by Donald Trump himself — not as president, but as a former donor.

During the 2015 campaign, Trump **bragged openly** that politicians from both parties regularly approached him for donations. And he gave — not out of altruism, but because it bought leverage.

"When they call, I give," Trump said during a Republican primary debate. *"And you know what? When I need something from them... they are there for me."*

This was not a scandal — it was a **selling point**. Trump framed it as proof that he **knew the game** because he had **played it**, and therefore could expose it.

What he unintentionally revealed was the **entire architecture of modern influence**: that access is bought, not earned, and that donations are not expressions of belief — they are **transactions in waiting**.

Trump was not unique. He was simply the first candidate to **say it out loud.**

This is the system *Citizens United* helped fortify — not corruption in the illegal sense, but **legalized influence**, where wealth grants you a megaphone and a seat at the table, while ordinary citizens watch through soundproof glass.

THE SCALIA CONTRAST: ORIGINALISM MEETS MODERN CAPITAL

One of the most surprising elements of the ruling was the alignment of **Justice Antonin Scalia**, a committed originalist, with the majority.

Scalia argued that the First Amendment was not intended to limit **who may speak**, only that **speech may not be abridged** by the government. He dismissed concerns about corporate personhood, writing:

"The identity of the speaker is not decisive in determining whether speech is protected."

This interpretation, while legally consistent with Scalia's textualist philosophy, **clashed with the Founders' warnings about undue influence.** Jefferson, Madison, and even Washington repeatedly warned of **factions**, **corporate charters**, and **wealthy special interests** dominating public institutions.

Scalia's view may have been correct in legal form, but it **missed the functional consequences** — how speech behaves when scaled by money, and how influence eclipses consent in a society where voice is priced.

LONG-TERM IMPLICATIONS FOR DEMOCRACY —

Citizens United didn't merely change campaign finance law. It:

- **Normalized plutocratic influence** in every election
- **Weakened public confidence** in representative government
- **Deepened polarization**, as campaigns became driven by emotional appeals funded by interest groups
- **Amplified nationalization**, pushing local candidates to align with national donor agendas
- **Undermined reform efforts**, as any regulation of corporate influence can now be framed as censorship

Over time, the ruling has not made speech freer — it has made it **less equal**.

A government "of the people, by the people, for the people" has become a **government shaped by the highest bidder**, with little regard for geography, class, or conscience.

CONCLUSION: THE FINAL SHIFT ——————

Citizens United did not collapse the republic. But it **sealed the transformation** that began in 1913.

- The 17th Amendment disconnected the states from federal representation.
- The 16th Amendment gave Washington access to private income.
- The Federal Reserve enabled limitless borrowing.
- PACs privatized the messaging of politics.
- Citizens United **legalized the consolidation of power by wealth**.

What began as a compound republic — with balance among people, states, and institutions — has become **a centralized system of managed consent**, shaped by corporations and billionaires, broadcast through paid influence, and codified by a Supreme Court ruling that mistook **freedom of speech** for **freedom of spending**.

In the next chapter, we will trace how this cycle — from 1913 to Citizens United — forms a **closed loop of control**, consolidating power across political, financial, and cultural lines over a 100-year arc.

That arc can be broken — but only if we first acknowledge it exists.

CHAPTER 6

The Cycle of Control – 1913 to 2013

"Liberty is never unalienable; it must be redeemed regularly with the blood of patriots or it always vanishes."

— William F. Buckley Jr.

Over the course of a single century — from 1913 to 2013 — the United States underwent a profound transformation. It did not happen through a singular revolution, coup, or war. It unfolded incrementally, legally, and often in the name of progress. But by 2013, the result was clear: **the carefully calibrated republic created in 1787 had given way to a centralized, corporatized, and finance-driven system of control**.

This century-long arc was not random. It followed a pattern — a closed loop in which **political power enabled financial power, and financial power, in turn, consolidated political control**. What emerged was a system neither fully public nor fully private, but **a hybrid ruling structure** in which elections were rituals, laws were commodities, and representation was more branding than accountability.

In this chapter, we will trace that arc — the rise of a **managerial elite**, the erosion of the **middle class and local governance**, and the replacement of **citizen-legislators with professional proxies**, loyal not to their states or voters but to donors and data firms.

FROM 1913: THE BEGINNING OF THE CYCLE ———

We began this story in Chapter 3, where 1913 marked the convergence of three foundational changes:

- The **16th Amendment** created a permanent federal income tax
- The **17th Amendment** severed the Senate from state legislatures
- The **Federal Reserve Act** privatized the nation's monetary policy

These changes didn't just expand federal authority — they **rerouted the flow of political and financial energy** in the American system. Power, once dispersed across states, classes, and institutions, began to concentrate in Washington, D.C. — and behind it, **Wall Street and global finance**.

From that point forward, the federal government could:

- Extract wealth from individuals directly
- Borrow endlessly from a private central bank
- Operate without significant input or resistance from the states

It was, in essence, the **constitutional enclosure of the commons** — a privatization of the original structure designed to preserve liberty through balance.

POST–WORLD WAR CONSOLIDATION AND COLD WAR CONTROL

The aftermath of World War I and especially World War II accelerated this trend. Massive military mobilization, war bonds, and federal contracts created an economic dependency on centralized decision-making.

The Cold War only intensified the effect. To defeat communism abroad, we built a **permanent war economy at home**:

- The rise of the **military-industrial complex**, warned against by Eisenhower
- Increased surveillance, intelligence, and federal administrative powers
- Alignment between defense contractors, media, and policy

In the name of national security, **a technocratic class emerged** — unelected, largely unaccountable, but deeply influential. What began as emergency powers became permanent infrastructure.

These bureaucracies — from the Pentagon to the CIA to HUD and the EPA — often operated **outside of legislative control**, guided more by regulation, executive order, and classified priorities than by the Constitution.

Local governance — once the heart of American civic life — became **increasingly irrelevant** in the face of national mandates, federal grant conditions, and preemption laws.

THE DISPLACEMENT OF THE MIDDLE CLASS ——

Perhaps the most tragic result of the 100-year arc was the **systematic displacement of the American middle class** — the very demographic that once anchored the republic.

From 1945 to roughly 1975, the U.S. middle class enjoyed unprecedented growth:

- Wages tracked productivity
- Home ownership soared
- Local institutions — churches, school boards, rotary clubs — held real influence

But starting in the 1980s, cracks appeared:

- Globalization sent manufacturing jobs overseas
- Financial deregulation enabled asset bubbles and predatory lending
- Real wages stagnated, even as corporate profits exploded

Each of these shifts was accompanied by **policy decisions made far from the reach of ordinary Americans** — often influenced or outright written by the same industries that profited from them.

The collapse of local economic autonomy mirrored the collapse of local political relevance. Mayors and city councils were increasingly powerless in the face of:

- Federal zoning restrictions
- EPA or DOE regulations
- Corporate land deals negotiated at the state or federal level

The middle class was not simply "left behind." It was **outsourced, overregulated, and politically disenfranchised** — not by accident, but by a century of intentional structural change.

THE EMERGENCE OF THE CORPORATE LEGISLATOR

As wealth consolidated, so too did political power. By the late 20th century, Congress was no longer filled with **citizen-legislators** —

farmers, doctors, shopkeepers serving short terms and returning home. It became a **professional political class**, many of whom:

- Never held jobs outside politics, consulting, or law
- Relied on permanent campaign operations and donor networks
- Traded legislation for future board seats, speaking gigs, or consulting contracts

This class is bipartisan, technocratic, and often indistinguishable in priorities. While they debate fiercely on social issues and media optics, their **donor bases are often identical**, and their loyalty lies not with districts but with data teams, fundraisers, and media strategists.

The legislator has become a **proxy** — a polished face reading from a script written elsewhere:

- Healthcare policy shaped by insurance lobbyists
- Tax policy crafted by Big Four accounting firms
- Environmental laws balanced against energy PAC funding

This was the final piece of the 100-year cycle: the replacement of **representation with performance**, and of **deliberation with data analytics**.

A SYSTEM THAT SUSTAINS ITSELF ————————

The system built over the last century is **not merely broken — it is self-reinforcing**.

- **Politicians** are elected through donations and media.
- **Media** thrives on election cycles and ad revenue.
- **Corporations** fund the campaigns and gain favorable policy.
- **Bureaucracies** enforce those policies through regulation, often written by the same firms.

All of this is sustained by:

- A tax system that funds centralization
- A monetary system that monetizes debt
- An electoral system that favors incumbents and high-spending candidates

It is a loop — **not a conspiracy, but a structure**.

And like any structure, it can be dismantled — but only if it is understood.

[1913: Fed / Income Tax / 17th Amd] →
[Centralized Money] →
[Centralized Politics] →
[Corporate Influence] →
[Privatized Speech] →

[PACs & Citizens United] →
[Election Manipulation] →
[Legislative Capture] →
[Policy for Donors] →
[Reinforced Federal Control] →
[Repeat Cycle]

A REPUBLIC DISMANTLED, QUIETLY ———————

The Founders did not fear one election, one crisis, or one corrupt man. They feared a **slow erosion of structure** — where ambition would no longer be checked, and where institutions designed for resistance would become instruments of control.

That erosion has occurred.

- The Senate no longer checks federal expansion — it enables it.
- The Fed no longer prevents economic panic — it engineers booms and busts.
- Elections no longer clarify the public will — they manufacture it.

From 1913 to 2013, America experienced not a political shift, but a **structural inversion**. The parts still look familiar — a Congress, a judiciary, a president. But the function has changed.

The republic — if we define it as a system of **citizen-led, state-balanced, constitutionally constrained governance** — no longer exists.

CONCLUSION: RECOGNIZING THE ARC TO BREAK IT

To restore what was lost, we must first **trace the arc**.

It is not enough to oppose a bad policy or a corrupt official. We must **understand the system that produces them**. From taxation to spending, from elections to lawmaking, from central banking to campaign finance, the American system has become **internally closed**, resilient not in liberty but in inertia.

This book is not about despair. It is about clarity. And in the chapters ahead, we will begin to explore **what must change — and how to begin changing it.**

Because only by understanding the **cycle**, can we begin the **reformation**.

CHAPTER 7

Breaking the Cycle – Reforming from the Ground Up

"The Constitution is not a suicide pact. But neither is it a license for tyranny."

— Thomas Sowell

"The machinery of government is broken — and it was designed that way."

— Anonymous former Senate staffer

For more than 100 years, the American political system has evolved into a **closed-loop machine** — where money, influence, and institutional capture ensure that meaningful reform is not merely difficult, but **structurally obstructed**.

It's easy to say "vote them out," "drain the swamp," or "take back the country." But for those who have tried, the path is littered with roadblocks:

- Candidates are crushed by Super PACs.
- Lawsuits are buried in process and precedent.
- Ballot measures are voided by judicial intervention.
- Investigations stall, commissions whitewash, and the press moves on.

This chapter explores the **hard truth**: the system is designed **not to be reformed**.

But that does not mean it is immune to **pressure, lawsuits, and structural disruption** — especially from below.

THE POWER STRUCTURE PROTECTS ITSELF ——

To understand why reform is so difficult, we must first acknowledge how **deep and wide the control runs**.

The elite interests who benefit from the current system do not merely **influence legislation** — they **control the gatekeepers** at every level:

- **The President** is elected via a donor-driven media system. Even insurgents must operate within donor-funded parties.

- **The Senate** — once a state-appointed body meant to check federal overreach — is now itself a product of nationalized PAC warfare.
- **The Judiciary** is appointed by those same presidents and confirmed by those same Senators. Even lower courts follow this same path — political screening disguised as merit.

But it doesn't stop at the federal level.

In the modern American city, even **local governance has been hijacked**:

- **City Managers**, not mayors, run the day-to-day operations in thousands of municipalities across the U.S.
- These city managers are **unelected technocrats**, often selected by corporate-friendly councils or "consultants" tied to regional development groups.
- Mayors are often **figureheads**, limited in power and **controlled by the same local PACs and developer networks** that dominate state politics.

State legislatures, secretaries of state, and election commissions have likewise become **arms of the machine**. They control the rules of the game:

- Who gets on the ballot
- Who oversees elections
- Who draws districts
- Who certifies results

This is not democracy. It is **managed democracy** — with the illusion of choice, bounded by invisible walls of procedure, funding, and control.

THE FRUSTRATION OF REFORMERS

Those who attempt to reform from inside the system soon find themselves neutralized:

- Outsider candidates are denied debate access, censored on platforms, or drowned in negative ad buys.
- Citizens proposing ballot initiatives are met with legal challenges funded by industry groups.
- Local referenda that pass are often **nullified by state preemption laws** or overruled by sympathetic courts.

It creates a sense of hopelessness.
And that is the **intended effect**.

When reform is systemically blocked, the public disengages. Disillusioned voters either check out or latch onto symbolic movements with no structural traction. This preserves the status quo.

But disengagement is not the only option.

There are cracks — **legal, structural, grassroots cracks** — that can still be widened.

TACTICAL RESISTANCE: SUING THE SYSTEM ——

One of the least explored — and most potent — methods of disruption is **suing the gatekeepers themselves**.

Most Americans assume election laws are untouchable, that campaign finance is protected by precedent, and that secretaries of state operate above the law.

That is not true.

Every Secretary of State, Election Commission, or PAC regulatory body operates under the **color of law** — which means **they can be sued** if they violate the Constitution or federal civil rights protections.

In a previous legal effort, I developed a suit — ready for filing in federal district court — to challenge:

- The **failure of election commissions to regulate Super PAC coordination**
- The **unconstitutional suppression of political speech** by limiting access to ballots and debates
- The **structural disenfranchisement of voters** under Citizens United and related decisions

The suit targets the **administrative functionaries** who enforce these rules — not the federal government directly, but the **state officers** and **commissions** who make enforcement decisions.

The legal grounds include:

- **42 U.S. Code § 1983** – for deprivation of civil rights under color of law
- **Equal Protection violations** – due to disparate treatment of candidates or political groups
- **First Amendment claims** – challenging the legal favoritism shown to PAC-funded candidates

This approach isn't a silver bullet.

But it creates **legal friction** — the system must defend itself, publicly, in court. It raises awareness, forces the production of evidence, and sometimes, **forces a ruling that cracks open precedent.**

One well-placed ruling — especially if appealed strategically — can threaten the foundation of campaign finance as it currently exists.

STATE-LEVEL PUSHBACK: WHERE THE REAL BATTLES BEGIN

Some of the most effective resistance has emerged not from Washington, but from **state constitutional amendments**, **ballot initiatives**, and **legislative nullification movements**.

Examples include:

- **South Dakota's 2016 Anti-Corruption Act**, which attempted to create public funding, lobbyist restrictions, and PAC transparency (later overturned by the legislature).
- **Missouri Amendment 1**, passed in 2018, to impose lobbying restrictions and independent redistricting.
- **Montana's attempts to ban corporate political expenditures** — struck down, but politically powerful.

States still hold **latent sovereignty** — and if coordinated, could:

- Mandate PAC transparency
- Ban dark money groups from contracting with state vendors
- Pass resolutions **calling for a new constitutional convention** under **Article V**

This last point — Article V — is a double-edged sword, but one that must be considered.

If 34 states call for a convention, Congress **must** convene one. And while the risks are high, **so is the potential** for:

- Reinstating state control of Senate appointments
- Overruling *Citizens United* via amendment
- Imposing term limits or campaign finance reforms

Even the **credible threat** of an Article V convention could force federal action.

LOCAL CONTROL:
THE FORGOTTEN BATTLEFIELD

While federal elections dominate headlines, the **local level** remains the most vulnerable — and the most crucial — space for change.

Even small actions here can disrupt the larger cycle:

- **County sheriffs** and **district attorneys** can refuse to enforce unconstitutional edicts
- **School boards** can reject federal funding tied to ideological mandates
- **City councils** can pass ordinances to **ban outside PAC influence** in local races

Many cities are now run by unelected **city managers**, creating a **technocratic firewall** between voters and decisions. But even city managers can be:

- Exposed through open records requests
- Replaced by charter amendments
- Stripped of power by legal restructuring

In Texas and other states, **home rule cities** allow extensive local control — if citizens choose to wield it.

The system counts on **your ignorance of your own power**.

BARRIERS TO ENTRY: PSYCHOLOGICAL AND INSTITUTIONAL

The elites understand that **most reformers give up early** — not because they are wrong, but because the cost of resistance is high:

- Legal fees
- Media attacks
- Political retaliation
- Smear campaigns
- Regulatory harassment

These aren't theoretical. They happen every cycle.

This is why change must come not from **lone actors**, but from **networked communities** — legally armed, digitally aware, and **willing to play the long game**.

This book is one tool among many — but you will need:

- Legal allies (civil liberties attorneys, constitutional experts)
- Technical allies (data miners, coders, media specialists)
- Financial allies (grassroots donors, alternative platforms)
- Tactical allies (local officeholders, law enforcement, watchdogs)

Change requires more than protest. It requires **structure**.

And that begins **city by city, county by county, state by state**.

A FRAMEWORK FOR RECLAIMING POWER ——————

Here is a rough sketch of the action map:

Domain	Tactic
Courts	File strategic 1983 suits against state actors or commissions
Ballot Access	Reform laws; sue for equal treatment in primaries and debates
PAC Transparency	Enact state/local disclosure requirements
Education	Publish open-source legal and civic training resources
City Government	Replace city manager systems with accountable executive models
Elections	Elect reformers to Secretary of State roles, county commissions
State Legislatures	Push nullification and Article V resolutions
Media	Build alternative, transparent news distribution infrastructure

CHAPTER 8

Toward a New Republic – Building a Parallel Structure of Liberty

"We must, indeed, all hang together, or most assuredly we shall all hang separately."

— Benjamin Franklin

"You never change things by fighting the existing reality. To change something, build a new model that makes the existing model obsolete."

— Buckminster Fuller

For over a century, Americans have tried to **fix a system designed to resist repair**. But now the time has come not just to **challenge the corrupted structure**, but to **build a parallel one** — one rooted in the principles of liberty, representation, and accountability.

This chapter lays out a vision for that new structure. Not a revolution in the streets, but a **reformation in the systems** — law by law, court by court, county by county. A **parallel republic**, rooted in the Constitution, grown through local control, and scaled by cooperation, not conquest.

THE NEED FOR PARALLEL STRUCTURES

The Founders never intended for the federal government to hold monopoly power over American life. The Constitution they ratified was **federalist**, not centralist. States were to be laboratories of liberty, and local communities were to handle most matters of governance.

That vision has been lost.

Today, the **centralized federal apparatus** — executive agencies, unelected regulators, subsidized media, and judicial fiat — has created a system where:

- **Policy flows downward**, from federal agencies to states to counties to citizens
- **Consent is presumed**, not requested
- **Power is exercised remotely**, not locally

Reclaiming the republic requires **decoupling** from this top-down system.

But how?

By building **parallel structures** that exist **within the law** — but **outside the influence** of the existing power architecture.

This is not sedition. It is self-governance.

THE FOUR PILLARS OF A PARALLEL REPUBLIC –

To functionally replace corrupt or captured institutions, we need structures that can:

1. **Enforce the law justly**
2. **Communicate truthfully**
3. **Govern locally**
4. **Fund transparently**

Each pillar reinforces the others. Together, they form the backbone of a **bottom-up republic**, one immune to federal capture because its legitimacy and functionality come **from the people**, not from the top.

Let's explore each one.

1. Parallel Law: Constitutional Enforcement at the County Level

The federal government cannot control 3,000+ counties **if counties assert their rights**.

- **Constitutional Sheriffs**: Law enforcement officers elected by the people, not appointed by federal agencies. They can **refuse to enforce unconstitutional orders**, from gun grabs to surveillance mandates.
- **County Nullification**: Local ordinances can nullify state or federal overreach. This was the strategy used by **sanctuary cities**, and it can be flipped — for **Second Amendment sanctuaries**, **free speech zones**, and more.
- **Local Grand Juries**: Re-establish grand juries independent of DA control to **investigate corruption**, enforce oaths of office, and subpoena officials.

The Constitution is not suspended at the county line. It can be enforced from the bottom up — if we have **citizens trained and willing** to hold their officials to it.

2. Parallel Communication: Ending the Information Monopoly

The regime maintains power through **narrative control**.

Legacy media, Big Tech platforms, and government "disinformation boards" work in unison to:

- Suppress independent thought
- Label dissent as extremism
- Promote federal policy as moral obligation

To resist this, we must build **a communications infrastructure that they do not control**:

- **Decentralized news outlets**: County- or state-level digital newspapers, podcasts, and AM radio networks
- **Open-source social platforms**: Not reliant on Silicon Valley servers or app store approval
- **Citizen journalist networks**: Equipped to document public meetings, record corruption, and publish FOIA records
- **Legal defense funds**: For those de-platformed or sued for exercising free speech

Freedom of the press is meaningless if only six conglomerates own the presses. The solution is not censorship, but **competition** — narrative by narrative, truth by truth.

3. *Parallel Governance: County Charters, Home Rule, and Networked Autonomy*

The ultimate answer to centralized control is **localized self-governance**.

States already contain the legal frameworks to govern from below — we simply fail to use them.

- **Home Rule Cities**: In states like Texas, home rule allows cities over a certain population to create their own charters. This means they can reject city managers, impose PAC bans, and require referenda for major spending.
- **County Councils of Governments**: Alternative governance bodies that work **across jurisdictions** — but are formed by **citizen vote**, not federal grants.

- **Townships and Special Districts**: Instead of lobbying a distant Congress, citizens can **create their own authorities** — for education, water, emergency services — free from federal strings.
- **State Compacts**: Multiple states can enter into agreements under the Constitution to **coordinate on shared interests**, from border enforcement to media standards.

We must move from a posture of begging for reform to **assuming control where it is legally permitted** — and then expanding that control through example and replication.

4. Parallel Finance: Ending Dependence on Federal Funds and Corporate PACs

No institution is truly sovereign if it depends on **hostile funding**.

The current system thrives because:

- Cities and counties are addicted to **federal grants with ideological strings**
- Candidates depend on **PAC money** for viability
- Local governments issue **bonds backed by Wall Street** to fund services

This financial dependence **creates political obedience**.

To break free:

- **Create community PACs** that fund candidates beholden to constituents, not corporations
- **Use local credit unions and blockchain-based ledgers** for transparency in public finance
- **Leverage local currencies and barter networks** in areas affected by federal overreach
- **Pass ordinances requiring budget referenda** — so no bond debt is created without direct voter approval

Parallel finance is not utopian. It is already happening — in homesteader communities, Amish regions, and sovereign tribes. It can happen in your county — with 10 committed citizens and a legal strategy.

A NEW CULTURE OF LIBERTY

Political structures without culture collapse. So we must **embed the republic in daily life**.

This means:

- **Teaching civics again** — real civics, not sanitized scripts
- **Mentoring youth in the principles of liberty**
- **Celebrating oaths of office and public service**
- **Creating ceremony and identity** around constitutional values

It may sound small. But the reason elites win is because they make **obedience cultural** — through media, schools, language, and ritual.

We must do the same for **resistance**.

DIGITAL SOVEREIGNTY AND TECH INFRASTRUCTURE

One of the most important components of a parallel republic is **digital independence**:

- Self-hosted email and document servers
- Distributed file storage and encrypted chat
- Volunteer-run voter databases
- Election monitoring tools
- Secure public forums and candidate vetting sites

Digital warfare is **information warfare**, and if the opposition can **shut down your bank account, your server, or your livestream**, you are no longer free.

We need parallel tools **designed for liberty**, not surveillance.

EXAMPLES ALREADY IN MOTION ——————

This isn't theory. It's happening:

- In **Shasta County, California**, the Board of Supervisors voted to terminate Dominion voting contracts and restore paper ballots.
- In **Florida**, local sheriffs have declared they will not enforce unconstitutional federal gun laws.
- In **Tarrant County, Texas**, activists have used public records laws to expose local corruption and flip council seats.
- In **New Hampshire**, the Free State Project has created an entire infrastructure of liberty-focused governance and education.

What these examples show is that **a determined minority of engaged citizens** can **reclaim governance — lawfully and effectively**.

FROM PARALLEL TO PRECEDENT ——————

The goal of building parallel structures is not merely survival. It is **replacement**.

As these systems grow and demonstrate success:

- **Other counties replicate them**
- **States acknowledge them**
- **Federal actors find themselves outpaced and irrelevant**

And when the moment comes — when the old system collapses under its own weight — there is a **ready alternative**, not chaos.

That is what makes this revolution not just moral, but strategic.

CONCLUSION: REBUILDING WITHOUT PERMISSION

We must accept a difficult truth:
The Republic our ancestors built no longer exists as designed.
But the soil of that Republic still holds the seeds.

We do not need permission from Washington, PACs, or courts to plant them.
We need only the courage to act, and the structure to succeed.

This chapter is your blueprint.

In the chapters that follow, we will expand each of these pillars into actionable campaigns — legal, electoral, digital, and cultural — backed by history, guided by law, and animated by the spirit of liberty that never dies, only waits to be awakened.

CHAPTER 9

The Doctrine of Consent – Reclaiming Sovereignty

"Governments are instituted among Men, deriving their just powers from the consent of the governed."

— Declaration of Independence (1776)

"The Constitution has no inherent authority or obligation. It has no authority or obligation at all, unless as a contract between man and man."

— Lysander Spooner

"All tyranny needs to gain a foothold is for people of good conscience to remain silent."

— Thomas Jefferson (attributed)

America was not founded on blind obedience.

It was founded on a **principle of conditional allegiance**: that government is legitimate only when it operates **with the consent of the governed**.

This single phrase — embedded in the Declaration of Independence — carries more legal, philosophical, and spiritual weight than entire volumes of modern legislation.

It is the root of the Republic.
And it is the standard by which we now judge its failure.

CONSENT IS NOT PERMANENT

Consent is not a one-time contract. It is a **living agreement**, renewed only as long as:

- The government operates within its delegated powers
- The governed retain meaningful voice and recourse
- The law applies equally, transparently, and justly

When these conditions fail — as they now have — the agreement is void.

This is not radicalism. It is **originalism**, as stated plainly by the Founders:

"Whenever any Form of Government becomes destructive of these ends, it is the Right of the People to alter or to abolish it."

— Declaration of Independence

To modern ears, "abolish" sounds extreme. But to the Framers, it was the default response to tyranny — not merely a right, but a **duty**.

"It is their right, it is their duty, to throw off such Government, and to provide new Guards for their future security."

This duty did not expire in 1776.
It persists — dormant, but potent.

COMPACT THEORY VS. NATIONAL SUPREMACY —

The American republic was born of a **compact** — a voluntary agreement between sovereign states and the people who delegated powers to their governments.

This is the **Compact Theory of the Constitution**, championed by Jefferson and Madison:

- The states created the federal government.
- The federal government has only those powers expressly delegated to it.

- The states — and by extension, the people — have the right to **interpose**, **nullify**, or **secede** when those powers are abused.

This theory stood until the Civil War, when Abraham Lincoln asserted a new model: **national supremacy** — the belief that the Union was indivisible, perpetual, and that federal authority overrides state and individual sovereignty.

This shift was never ratified by amendment. It was **enforced by war**.

And though the Union remained intact, the principle of consent was **forever undermined**.

Today, that tension remains unresolved:

- Do states have the right to say no?
- Do people have the right to resist, withdraw, or nullify?
- Is the federal government a servant, or a master?

The modern administrative state functions on the **Lincoln model** — centralized, permanent, and beyond recall. But the Constitution still speaks the language of compact and consent.

And so must we.

NULLIFICATION AS AN EXPRESSION OF CONSENT

Nullification is not rebellion.

It is **the most peaceful form of resistance** available in a constitutional republic.

It simply means: *We do not consent to this law here.*

Jefferson called it "the rightful remedy" to federal overreach. Madison defended it in the **Virginia Resolution**. Entire states used it to defy:

- Federal censorship laws in the 1790s
- Fugitive slave laws in the 1850s
- Draft laws during the Civil War
- Prohibition in the 1920s
- Immigration mandates in the 2000s

Today, progressives nullify federal drug laws and ICE directives.

Conservatives nullify federal gun restrictions and vaccine mandates.

Nullification, when exercised lawfully and locally, is a form of **civil consent withdrawal**.

It says: *This community does not give you power here.*

That principle is the core of liberty. And it must be revived — not in theory, but in action.

THE MORAL CASE FOR RESISTANCE

There comes a point when obedience is no longer virtue, but cowardice.

When compliance is not peacekeeping, but **complicity**.

That point arrives when:

- Laws are passed without representation
- Courts rule by ideology, not constitutionality
- Elections are rigged by procedure and finance
- Free speech is punished, not protected
- Government exists to protect itself, not the people

In that moment — this moment — resistance is not only justified. It is **morally necessary**.

"Disobedience to tyrants is obedience to God."

— Benjamin Franklin (motto on his proposed seal for the United States)

"An unjust law is no law at all."

— St. Augustine, revived by Martin Luther King, Jr.

This is not a call to violence.
It is a call to **moral clarity**.

It means suing when silenced.
It means refusing to enforce unconstitutional edicts.
It means forming your own structures — media, schools, courts, councils — when the existing ones betray their purpose.

LYSANDER SPOONER AND THE CONSTITUTIONAL DILEMMA

No discussion of consent is complete without acknowledging **Lysander Spooner**, the 19th-century abolitionist and constitutional philosopher.

Spooner argued that the Constitution had no inherent authority unless each person explicitly consented to it — and that consent could not be presumed across generations.

He wrote:

"But whether the Constitution really be one thing, or another, this much is certain – that it has either authorized such a government as we have had, or has been powerless to prevent it."

Spooner was not anti-American. He was pro-sovereignty.

He believed in natural rights, voluntary association, and **explicit consent** — not inherited obligation.

His solution?

- Return to a system where individuals and communities **freely choose** their governance.
- Reject systems where force replaces legitimacy.

Spooner's radical honesty is needed now more than ever.

QUOTES THAT FRAME THE FIGHT

"That government is best which governs least."

— Thomas Jefferson

"No man is good enough to govern another man without that other's consent."

— Abraham Lincoln (before he abandoned the idea in practice)

"Those who make peaceful revolution impossible will make violent revolution inevitable."

— John F. Kennedy

"The liberties of our country, the freedom of our civil Constitution, are worth defending at all hazards."

— Samuel Adams

"We are reduced to the alternative of choosing an unconditional submission to the tyranny of irritated ministers, or resistance by force."

— Declaration of the First
Continental Congress (1774)

The arc of American resistance is not one of destruction, but **reclamation** — reclaiming the idea that power flows upward, not down.

HOW TO REASSERT CONSENT IN PRACTICE

Here are practical ways to express **nonviolent withdrawal of consent**:

Domain	Action
Elections	Sue for ballot access, equal debate rules, or PAC exclusion
Local Law	Pass ordinances nullifying federal intrusion (e.g., gun rights, zoning)
Civic Engagement	Hold referenda, town halls, and oaths of office ceremonies
Education	Build parallel school boards, homeschool co-ops, and civics groups

Domain	Action
Law Enforcement	Elect sheriffs who will refuse to enforce unlawful orders
Courts	Assert jury nullification rights and use grand juries against corruption
Finance	Reject federal grants with ideological strings; build local credit unions
Media	Create community news networks independent of corporate control

These are not symbolic. They are **lawful acts of sovereignty**.

Each one reclaims a piece of your consent.

CONCLUSION: THE REPUBLIC OF THE FUTURE MUST BE CHOSEN

The great irony of our time is this:

The Founders gave us the tools to resist — and we've been trained not to use them.

We were taught that elections are the only voice we have.
That law is what courts say it is.
That justice is whatever Washington allows.

That is not America.
That is **Empire**, wearing a tricorn hat.

The future Republic — if there is to be one — will not come from Washington, or even from the states.

It will come from **a million small acts of lawful, moral resistance**.

From citizens who say:

"No, I do not consent."

And who then build something better in its place.

CHAPTER 10

A New American Covenant

"The Constitution is not a suicide pact."

— Justice Robert H. Jackson

"We mutually pledge to each other our Lives, our Fortunes and our sacred Honor."

— Declaration of Independence (1776)

"The truth is that liberty is not bestowed by governments; it is claimed by men and women with the courage to keep it."

— Anonymous veteran, written
in the margin of a Bible

There comes a moment in every generational struggle where resistance must become **rebuilding**, where dissent must become **design**.

This is that moment.

We have spent this book examining what went wrong — the laws, the amendments, the courts, the campaigns, and the capture. But now we must answer a deeper question:

What are we for?

Not just against oligarchy. Not just against corruption. Not just against elite control.

But **for** something. Something enduring. Something binding. Something worthy of passing on.

WHAT WE'RE FOR

We are for a **Constitutional Republic**, in the truest, oldest, and most radical sense — one where:

- **Families** are sovereign units, not state-controlled dependents
- **Faith** is practiced freely and without persecution, even if it offends
- **Truth** is spoken without fear, and the consequences of honesty are borne with honor
- **Justice** is not selective or political, but blind and righteous
- **Local loyalty** matters more than distant power
- **Oaths mean something** — and breaking them is a form of treason

We are for **representation**, not manipulation.

For **service**, not rule.

For **liberty**, not comfort.

For **truth**, even when it costs.

That is the new covenant.

Not written by elites in ivory towers, but by citizens in garages, churches, libraries, and county halls.

FAMILY IS THE FIRST GOVERNMENT

The family is the first institution — before the state, before the church, before the school.

It is where order, love, discipline, and belief are formed.

The regime knows this, which is why it attacks the family with:

- Economic pressure (housing, inflation, taxation)
- Cultural rot (porn, nihilism, sterilization)
- Legal interference (CPS overreach, schooling mandates, custody laws)

To restore the Republic, we must **restore the family**.

This means:

- Mothers and fathers with courage and presence
- Children raised in truth, not propaganda
- Generational memory passed down, not outsourced
- Meals shared. Books read. Prayers spoken.

There is no stronger political act than **raising children to love truth and hate tyranny**.

The new American covenant begins at the dinner table.

FAITH IS THE CORNERSTONE OF LIBERTY ———

A people without God cannot remain free.

This is not merely a theological claim — it is a civic truth.

If rights do not come from the Creator, they come from the State. And what the State gives, it can take away.

Faith is not a private hobby. It is **a public anchor**.

It reminds us:

- We are not owned by the government
- We answer to a higher law
- We are not the center of history — we are stewards of it

In every moment of American renewal — from Valley Forge to Selma — faith was the fire that kept the lamp burning.

The new covenant must be built on that flame again.

OATHS TO ONE ANOTHER

The Founders pledged lives, fortunes, and honor.
What are we willing to pledge?

It must start with **a civic declaration** — not to a party or candidate, but to each other.

Let us write it plainly:

"We, the citizens of these United States, bound by law, heritage, and shared purpose, do pledge our lives and labor to restore constitutional government, to defend liberty from all enemies foreign and domestic, and to pass on to our children a republic worthy of the name."

"We reject the corruption of moneyed influence, the false promises of tyranny, and the silencing of truth. We will teach. We will protect. We will build. And if we must, we will stand alone."

"But we will never consent to our own enslavement."

This is more than rhetoric. It is an oath. And like all oaths, it must be kept — even when it hurts.

TEACH. PROTECT. BUILD. ENDURE. ————————

These are the four tasks of the remnant — those who still believe the Republic is worth saving.

Teach

- History, real and unfiltered
- Law, as written
- Rights, as inherited
- Tactics, as tested

Every household a schoolhouse. Every citizen a historian. Every conversation a lesson in liberty.

Protect

- Families from cultural and state assault
- Churches from political pressure
- Communities from financial dependency
- Truth from extinction

If you do not protect your own, they will be taken from you — slowly, legally, and permanently.

Build

- Local structures: councils, credit unions, patrols, courts
- Independent media and communications

- Parallel economies and governance

We must replace what we no longer trust — not protest it, but **out-create it**.

Endure

- Smears, bans, audits, arrests
- Isolation, betrayal, fear
- Loss, failure, setback

The regime has more power. We must have more courage.

Endurance is what separates moments from movements.

A REPUBLIC YOU CAN HOLD IN YOUR HANDS ⸺

The next republic will not be televised.
It will be lived, taught, and defended block by block.

You will not need to wait for permission.
You will not need to run for office.
You will not need to win the internet.

You will only need a few good men and women — in your county, on your street, under your roof — who are **willing to be free**.

You will need the courage to say:

- Not in my town.
- Not to my children.
- Not with my silence.

And when you say that, you'll find you're not alone.

CONCLUSION: PLEDGING SACRED HONOR AGAIN

We began this book in mourning — for a Republic lost, for a Constitution desecrated, for a people deceived.

We end it with a vow — not to restore the old, but to build the new on the foundations of the eternal.

The Constitution is not a perfect document. But it remains the **greatest civic covenant** ever written by free men.

It deserves defenders.
It deserves successors.
It deserves **you**.

> *"I know not what course others may take, but as for me, give me liberty or give me death."*

> — Patrick Henry

"The battle, sir, is not to the strong alone; it is to the vigilant, the active, the brave."

Let us be brave. Let us be faithful. Let us be free.

And let us teach our children to do the same.

End of Chapter 10: A New American Covenant

APPENDIX A

Legal Citations and Source Notes

This appendix provides expanded footnotes, historical legal references, and source excerpts used throughout the book *Subverting the Republic: How the 17th Amendment and Citizens United Corrupted the Balance of American Government.*

1. THE FOUNDERS' DESIGN & ORIGINAL INTENT

Federalist Papers:

- **Federalist No. 10** (Madison): Warns against factions and emphasizes a large republic to check their influence.
- **Federalist No. 39** (Madison): Describes the compound republic structure, including the federal-state balance.
- **Federalist No. 51** (Madison): Explains checks and balances and the need for separation of powers.

U.S. Constitution, Article I, Section 3: Original method of selecting Senators by state legislatures.

James Madison's Notes on the Constitutional Convention (1787): Discusses the rationale for a bicameral legislature and indirect election of Senators.

2. THE 17TH AMENDMENT AND STATE SOVEREIGNTY

Text of the 17th Amendment (1913): Establishes direct election of U.S. Senators by the people.

Orren, Karen. "The U.S. Senate and the 17th Amendment: From Representative to Populist." Journal of American Political Thought, 2014.

Luther v. Borden, 48 U.S. (7 How.) 1 (1849): Limits federal courts from intervening in disputes over state governments' republican character.

3. FEDERAL RESERVE & INCOME TAX (1913)

16th Amendment Text (1913): Grants Congress power to levy income tax.

Federal Reserve Act (1913): Law creating the Federal Reserve System.

Pollock v. Farmers' Loan & Trust Co., 157 U.S. 429 (1895): Precursor to 16th Amendment, invalidated federal income tax as unconstitutional.

U.S. Code Title 12 - Banks and Banking: Codifies powers and structure of Federal Reserve.

G. Edward Griffin, *The Creature from Jekyll Island* (1994): Investigative history of Federal Reserve's founding.

4. CAMPAIGN FINANCE AND CITIZENS UNITED

Buckley v. Valeo, 424 U.S. 1 (1976): Upheld individual expenditure limits but struck down limits on candidate's own spending.

Citizens United v. FEC, 558 U.S. 310 (2010): Struck down restrictions on independent political expenditures by corporations.

Justice Stevens' Dissent (Citizens United): Emphasized the risk of corporate domination of the political process.

McCutcheon v. FEC, 572 U.S. 185 (2014): Removed aggregate contribution limits by individuals to political campaigns.

5. LEGAL DOCTRINES OF CONSENT AND SOVEREIGNTY

Declaration of Independence (1776): Core claim of government by consent of the governed.

Lysander Spooner, *No Treason: The Constitution of No Authority* (1867): Classic treatise on voluntary governance and constitutional legitimacy.

Federalist No. 46 (Madison): Discusses how states and the people can push back against federal overreach.

Thomas Jefferson, Kentucky Resolutions (1798): Argues for states' rights to nullify unconstitutional federal laws.

Printz v. United States, 521 U.S. 898 (1997): Limits federal commandeering of state officials.

6. NULLIFICATION, STATE RESISTANCE, AND LOCAL AUTONOMY

Gonzales v. Raich, 545 U.S. 1 (2005): Broad interpretation of the Commerce Clause; triggered renewed nullification efforts.

New York v. United States, 505 U.S. 144 (1992): Found federal mandate coercing states unconstitutional.

Alaska Firearms Freedom Act (2010): State law asserting that intrastate firearms are not subject to federal regulation.

Tenth Amendment Center (tenthamendmentcenter.com): Advocacy group tracking nullification bills and state sovereignty efforts.

7. HISTORICAL AND PHILOSOPHICAL SOURCES

Patrick Henry's Liberty Speech (1775): "Give me liberty or give me death!"

Thomas Paine, *Common Sense* (1776): Articulates the moral and practical arguments for independence.

John Locke, *Second Treatise of Government* (1689): Lays philosophical foundation for government by consent.

St. Augustine, *City of God* (426 AD): Source of "an unjust law is no law at all."

Martin Luther King Jr., *Letter from Birmingham Jail* (1963): Expands on the moral duty to resist unjust laws.

For full digital source archive, reference companion site: **[SubvertingTheRepublic.com/AppendixA]** (Coming soon).

APPENDIX B

Sample Legislation and Resolutions

This appendix provides model legal tools for restoring constitutional balance, enabling local, state, and federal actors to act independently of captured institutions. Included are draft bills, repeal resolutions, state sovereignty compacts, and a full sample federal lawsuit.

1. MODEL TERM-LIMITS BILL (STATE LEVEL)

Title: Citizen Accountability Term Limit Act

Section 1: Purpose

To establish term limits for members of the state legislature and U.S. Congress as a condition of ballot access.

Section 2: Definitions

- "Combined service" means total years served in either legislative chamber.

Section 3: Provisions

- No person shall serve more than 12 years combined in the State House and State Senate.
- No person shall be certified as a candidate for U.S. House or Senate if they have served more than 12 combined years in those offices.

Section 4: Enforcement

- The Secretary of State shall not certify ballot access for ineligible candidates.

Section 5: Severability

- If any portion of this Act is found unconstitutional, the remainder shall remain in effect.

2. 17TH AMENDMENT REPEAL RESOLUTION (STATE LEGISLATURE) ——————

Title: Resolution Calling for Repeal of the 17th Amendment

WHEREAS, The 17th Amendment eliminated the appointment of U.S. Senators by state legislatures, and thereby diminished state sovereignty;

WHEREAS, Direct election of Senators has resulted in nationalized campaigns, financial capture by PACs, and erosion of federalism;

BE IT RESOLVED, That the legislature of the State of [STATE] calls upon the United States Congress to propose a constitutional amendment repealing the 17th Amendment;

BE IT FURTHER RESOLVED, That certified copies of this resolution be sent to the Speaker of the House, the President of the Senate, and each member of Congress from this state.

3. STATE SOVEREIGNTY COMPACT TEMPLATE ——

Title: Interstate Compact for Constitutional State Sovereignty

Article I: Purpose

To reassert the Tenth Amendment rights of each participating state and establish mutual aid in resisting unconstitutional federal actions.

Article II: Creation

This Compact shall be entered into by two or more states adopting legislation in substantively identical form.

Article III: Commitments

- Each member state commits to review all federal legislation for constitutional compliance.
- Each member state agrees to decline enforcement of laws or mandates found unconstitutional.

Article IV: Enforcement

Member states may jointly initiate litigation or nullification proceedings.

Article V: Withdrawal

A member state may withdraw with 60 days written notice.

4. SAMPLE FEDERAL LAWSUIT (U.S. DISTRICT COURT) ─────────

IN THE UNITED STATES DISTRICT COURT

FOR THE NORTHERN DISTRICT OF TEXAS

PLAINTIFF: John Doe, individually and on behalf of all similarly situated voters

DEFENDANT: Texas Secretary of State, in official capacity

NATURE OF SUIT: Violation of First and Fourteenth Amendments; 42 U.S.C. §1983

COMPLAINT:

1. **Jurisdiction and Venue**: This Court has jurisdiction under 28 U.S.C. §1331 and 42 U.S.C. §1983.
2. **Parties**:
   - Plaintiff is a registered voter and taxpayer in the State of Texas.
   - Defendant is the chief election officer of the State of Texas.
3. **Statement of Facts**:
   - Plaintiff alleges that political speech and electoral access are being systematically distorted by PAC financing and ballot restrictions.

- Defendant enforces rules that favor major-party candidates and super PAC-aligned campaign structures.

4. **Claims for Relief:**
   - Violation of Equal Protection (Fourteenth Amendment)
   - Violation of Free Speech and Association (First Amendment)
   - Structural disenfranchisement via unconstitutional application of Citizens United

5. **Relief Requested:**
   - Declaratory judgment that current PAC-dominated financing regime violates constitutional rights
   - Injunctive relief requiring Secretary of State to create equal ballot access conditions
   - Costs and attorney fees under 42 U.S.C. §1988

Respectfully submitted,

[Plaintiff signature]

Pro se or with Counsel

These sample tools are offered as templates and should be reviewed and adapted in coordination with licensed counsel in the relevant jurisdiction.

APPENDIX C

FAQ and Talking Points for Reform Advocates

This appendix equips advocates with ready answers to common objections, quick reference facts for interviews or hearings, and principled talking points for town halls, social media, or legislative outreach.

TOP 10 OBJECTIONS AND ANSWERS

1. "Wasn't the 17th Amendment a good reform?"

Answer: It was well-intentioned, but it stripped states of their primary check on federal power. Instead of reducing corruption, it nationalized Senate campaigns and made senators beholden to donors, not legislatures.

2. "Isn't Citizens United just about free speech?"

Answer: Corporate money is not speech. *Citizens United* allowed unlimited political spending by artificial entities, drowning out the voice of individuals and distorting democratic participation.

3. "Don't PACs level the playing field?"

Answer: No. PACs entrench incumbents and amplify elite voices. Ordinary citizens cannot match their influence or access.

4. "Is this just a partisan issue?"

Answer: No. Corruption and centralization transcend party. Both Republicans and Democrats exploit the current system. This is a constitutional issue, not a partisan one.

5. "Wouldn't repealing the 17th Amendment be anti-democratic?"

Answer: No. It restores federalism — the right of states to be represented as sovereign entities. Senators would still be accountable — just to the people's representatives in the state house.

6. "Isn't the Supreme Court the final say?"

Answer: Courts interpret law, not create it. And they're not infallible. *Dred Scott*, *Plessy*, and *Korematsu* were all upheld by the Court. Citizens have the duty to resist unjust rulings.

7. "Nullification isn't legal."

Answer: States have always resisted federal overreach — from the Fugitive Slave Act to marijuana laws. Nullification is part of the American tradition of consent and compact.

8. "Isn't this too extreme?"

Answer: What's extreme is $10 billion elections, cities run by unelected managers, and kids being taught they have no rights. Reform is the moderate position.

9. "What can one person do?"

Answer: Everything. Every reform movement in U.S. history began with individuals — not institutions. Speak, write, organize, and act locally.

10. "Aren't we too far gone to fix this?"

Answer: Only if we do nothing. History is full of impossible turnarounds — America being one of them.

QUICK FACTS AND FIGURES ────────────────

- **1913:** The 16th, 17th Amendments and Federal Reserve Act passed within months of each other.
- **PACs:** Over $14 billion was spent in the 2020 election — more than double the 2016 cycle.
- **Citizens United (2010):** Triggered a 500% increase in outside spending in federal elections.
- **Senate incumbents:** Reelection rate over 85% — despite Congress's approval rating below 20%.
- **States with term limits (2023):** 15 states limit legislative terms; Congress has none.

TALKING POINTS FOR OUTREACH ────────────

- *"This isn't about left vs. right — it's about liberty vs. control."*
- *"If we don't reclaim state sovereignty, we don't have a republic — we have a province."*
- *"Every senator now represents Wall Street, not Main Street. That's not what the founders intended."*
- *"No corporation should have more political speech than a citizen."*
- *"We're not trying to burn it down — we're trying to rebuild it the way it was designed."*

Print and distribute this appendix at public events, legislative hearings, or constitutional training sessions. Pair with Appendix D (timeline visuals) for maximum clarity and impact.

APPENDIX D

The Closed Loop – Charting the 100-Year Arc

This appendix contains a visual timeline and diagrams detailing the century-long consolidation of political and financial control in the United States — from the foundational year of 1913 to the post–Citizens United landscape.

1. TIMELINE: KEY MILESTONES IN THE 100-YEAR ARC

1913

- 16th Amendment ratified (federal income tax established)
- 17th Amendment ratified (direct election of Senators)
- Federal Reserve Act passed (central banking created)

1933

- Glass-Steagall Act separates commercial and investment banking
- Executive Order 6102 confiscates private gold ownership

1944

- Bretton Woods Agreement ties global currency to the U.S. dollar

1971

- Nixon ends the gold standard (fiat currency fully adopted)

1974–1979

- FEC created post-Watergate
- Rise of PACs and campaign finance regulations

1996

- Telecommunications Act paves way for media consolidation

2002

- McCain-Feingold Campaign Reform Act (BCRA) temporarily curbs soft money

2010

- Citizens United v. FEC strikes down limits on independent political expenditures by corporations

2014

- McCutcheon v. FEC eliminates aggregate individual contribution limits

2020–Present

- Political campaigns exceed $14 billion in spending
- Record levels of Super PAC and 501(c)(4) dark money involvement
- Growing public distrust in institutions

2. FULL-PAGE INFOGRAPHIC (SEE VISUAL INSERT) ————————————————

Title: *The Closed System: 1913–2013*

Design Features:

- Three converging arcs: Taxation (16th), Representation (17th), and Banking (Fed)
- Overlaid with campaign finance spikes (2010–2020)

- Icons showing milestones in money flow, media consolidation, and legislative capture

Visual Headings:

- "Start of the Cycle" (1913)
- "Entrenchment Phase" (1933–1971)
- "Deregulation Phase" (1996–2010)
- "Capture Complete" (2010–Present)

3. DIAGRAM: CLOSED SYSTEM OF REPRESENTATION AND INFLUENCE

Step-by-Step Flowchart:

1. **Corporations & Donors**
   → Fund Super PACs and 501(c)(4)s
2. **Super PACs/501(c)(4)s**
   → Spend on ads, lobbying, candidate support
3. **Candidates/Elected Officials**
   → Win office with donor funding
   → Write policy favorable to donors
4. **Regulatory Capture**
   → Appointees from same industries regulate themselves
5. **Legislative Gridlock + State Preemption**
   → Real power shifts to unaccountable federal agencies and courts

6. **Citizens Disenfranchised**

    → Less representation, more dependence

7. **Cycle Reinforced**

    → New regulations written by captured institutions; repeat

This closed loop of influence illustrates the need for structural, not superficial, reform. Visuals from this appendix are ideal for presentations, public education, and legislative briefings.

THE CLOSED LOOP
CHARTING THE 100-YEAR ARC OF ELIT FINANCIAL INFLUENCE AND CONTROL

1913	**1974**	**1976**	**2010**
●	●	●	●
16th Amendment (Income Tax)	FECA Hen	*Buckley v.* Valeo	Citizens United
17th Amendment (Direct Senate Elections)			
Federal Reserve Act			

CLOSED SYSTEM OF REPRESENTATION AND MONEY FLOW

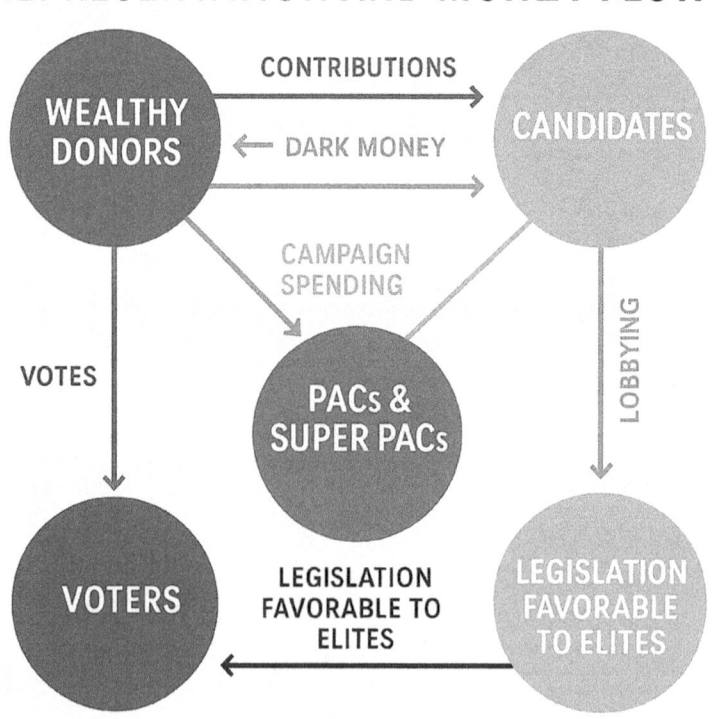

APPENDIX E

Model Legal Actions and Ballot Language

This appendix provides sample legal tools for individuals and advocacy groups to challenge systemic corruption, assert constitutional rights, and pursue electoral reform through direct democratic action.

1. FEDERAL CIVIL RIGHTS LAWSUIT TEMPLATE (42 U.S.C. §1983)

IN THE UNITED STATES DISTRICT COURT FOR THE [YOUR DISTRICT] DISTRICT OF [YOUR STATE]

PLAINTIFF: [Your Full Name], individually and on behalf of similarly situated voters

DEFENDANT: [Secretary of State or Election Commission Official], in official capacity

COMPLAINT:

1. **Jurisdiction and Venue:**
   - Jurisdiction lies under 28 U.S.C. §1331 and 42 U.S.C. §1983.
   - Venue is proper under 28 U.S.C. §1391.
2. **Parties:**
   - Plaintiff is a registered voter and resident of [county/state].
   - Defendant is responsible for the administration of state election laws.
3. **Factual Allegations:**
   - The current election system creates unequal access to ballot placement and debate inclusion based on financial structures.
   - Defendant enforces rules that favor major-party candidates aligned with PACs and corporate funders.
4. **Claims for Relief:**
   - Violation of First Amendment rights (free speech, free association)
   - Violation of Fourteenth Amendment (equal protection)
   - Injunctive relief to stop enforcement of discriminatory rules
5. **Relief Requested:**
   - Declaratory judgment
   - Injunction preventing further enforcement of exclusionary ballot rules
   - Legal costs under 42 U.S.C. §1988

Signed: [Your Name and Contact Information]

2. SAMPLE BALLOT INITIATIVE LANGUAGE – STATE TERM LIMITS

Ballot Title: Citizen-Led Term Limit Amendment

Ballot Summary: This amendment limits service in the state legislature to no more than 12 years total, whether in one chamber or combined.

Text: "No person may serve more than 12 years total in the state legislature. This includes any combination of service in the House and Senate. This provision applies to all terms beginning after the effective date of this amendment."

3. SAMPLE LOCAL ORDINANCE – PAC TRANSPARENCY

Title: Political Action Committee (PAC) Transparency Ordinance

Section 1: Registration Requirement

Any PAC operating within the jurisdiction must register with the city clerk and disclose:

- Primary funding sources
- List of expenditures above $200

Section 2: Expenditure Reporting

PACs must file monthly disclosures during election years and quarterly outside of them.

Section 3: Enforcement

Failure to comply results in a $1,000 fine per offense and disqualification from participating in local elections.

4. SAMPLE COUNTY RESOLUTION – FEDERAL NULLIFICATION

Title: County Resolution to Reject Unconstitutional Federal Mandates

WHEREAS, the Tenth Amendment reserves to the states and their subdivisions all powers not expressly delegated to the federal government;

WHEREAS, recent federal mandates in areas such as speech, medical autonomy, and firearms contradict constitutional protections;

BE IT RESOLVED, that the County of [Name] will not recognize, enforce, or allocate funds for the implementation of any federal action that infringes on constitutionally protected rights;

BE IT FURTHER RESOLVED, that all county employees and elected officials are directed to review all federal orders for constitutional compliance prior to enforcement.

These model texts may be freely adapted and distributed with credit to *Subverting the Republic* (2025). Consult local counsel for jurisdiction-specific formatting or filing requirements.

www.ingramcontent.com/pod-product-compliance
Lightning Source LLC
Chambersburg PA
CBHW061806120626
46550CB00005B/2153